AF208011

THE

MOTHER'S

BOOK

How to Survive the Molestation of Your Child

Third Edition

CAROLYN M. BYERLY

KENDALL/HUNT PUBLISHING COMPANY
4050 Westmark Drive   Dubuque, Iowa 52002

Typography and Layout: Evelyn Roehl, Flying Fingers, Seattle, WA

Copyright © 1985, 1992, 1997 by Carolyn M. Byerly

ISBN 0-7872-4326-4

All rights reserved. No part of this publication may be reproduced,
stored in a retrieval system, or transmitted, in any form or by any
means, electronic, mechanical, photocopying, recording, or otherwise,
without the prior written permission of the copyright owner.

Printed in the United States of America

10 9 8 7 6 5 4 3 2

Contents

Acknowledgments

Books are the work of many. Thanks to Lisa Cobus, Sonia Bouvier, Louise Miller, and other staff at the Task Force for Battered Women, in Ithaca, for all their help on this edition. To the women who came out on a cold Saturday morning in March to share their personal accounts of survival. To Marcia Cohn Spiegel and Carol Adams who were advisors to Marie Fortune on the religious issues chapter. To Marie Fortune and Muriel Templeton for their excellent, important chapters on religious issues and mothers' recovery. To Baoying Guo, my research assistant at Ithaca College, who collected library materials for me. To Lynn Crook for information on repressed memory cases. To Kay McGraw for personal support and feedback.

Also thanks to all the women and men who, through the years, have helped in one way or another to develop the ideas and information in this and earlier editions. To the mother survivors who call me out of the blue to talk after they've read the book, and, inevitably, to provide me with new insights. To Evelyn Roehl for design and typesetting yet another edition. To the whole crew at Kendall/Hunt Publishing Company for believing that *The Mother's Book* is a necessary resource and publishing it again and again. To the staff and board of the Center for the Prevention of Sexual and Domestic Violence for continuing to sponsor the book.

Others to be thanked include everyone who works daily to serve the victims and survivors of sexual and family violence, and stands up for them in the legal and helping service processes. Also, thanks to legislators who have had the guts to sponsor and argue for legislation that has vastly improved our statutes to protect children from sexual abuse and to enhance the likelihood that offenders would be prosecuted. To enlightened police and attorneys who have led the way legally. To Helan Smith for her courage and willingness to share what she knows. And, finally, to my late brother Robert, who has deepened my commitment to stop child sexual abuse.

Carolyn M. Byerly
Ithaca, New York
May 1997

Introduction

Women who have survived their children's sexual abuse have much to teach us about motherhood, personal difficulty, fortitude, and humanity. Mothers' statements and stories, therefore, play a central role in the shaping of this third edition of *The Mother's Book*, just as they have the earlier editions. Through the last twelve years, I have collected stories and other information from conversations with mothers by phone and in person; from letters, diaries, and press clippings; and during interviews and focus group meetings. Mothers' own statements, thus, serve as the backbone for the book, and they breathe life into the data and clinical information drawn from recently published sources.

While I draw from the rich experiences of women who have given so much of themselves to make this a better book, I also work to provide them confidentiality. The basic story lines are real, but names are changed and details of personal accounts used as examples to illustrate points in the book are sufficiently altered so that private lives remain just that.

The Mother's Book's natural first audience is women trying to cope with their children's molestation. However, because so little still has been published for or about mothers faced with this situation, the book inevitably serves a wider cross-section of users. Among this second group are victims and survivors who want to understand their mothers better; relatives, friends and co-workers of mothers; counselors and other helping professionals; prosecutors and other legal personnel; women's shelter and rape crisis center staff; and college students and faculty. The book sells in several nations and has a multicultural audience.

Women whose children are sexually abused need and deserve much understanding and support. Mothers of abused children are often stigmatized for what has occurred. I have seen mothers blamed by agency and police personnel for "letting this happen" to their children. Women caught in the tangled web of incestuous families find particular pain in such insinuations. Usually troubled by a range of family problems that may include their own abuse by the child's offender, such mothers feel a profound abandonment and helplessness. Not only are mothers sometimes blamed for the abuse, they are also typically left to carry the burden of solacing and caring for children and other family members in a stressful time. The attentions of police, prosecutors, lawyers, and counselors are on victim and offender, once disclosure occurs. Few hands are extended to help mothers with their practical chores, and few ears are open to listen to mothers talk about their own confusion, anger, or hurt.

It is important to address issues of responsibility in child sexual abuse. By and large, women cannot be blamed for the incidence of child sexual abuse. Reported incidence and research consistently show that men comprise the vast majority of sex offenders. When confronted with a child's sexual abuse, mothers typically want to protect their children from further abuse. Some are able to act immediately to do this, but some are uncertain of how to do this. Others are afraid to believe this terrible thing has happened, because in acknowledging the truth, they will have to stand up against the authority of their husbands (or other powerful figures) in ways they perhaps have never learned to do. Women who have their own histories of childhood sexual or physical assault may still feel powerless as adults; the child's sexual assault serves to retraumatize these mothers and render them as fearful and immobile as they were when their own victimization occurred years earlier.

Most common is the mother who knows *something* is wrong with her child but not *what* that something is. The child may begin to act in troubling ways—such as be given to angry outbursts, to masturbation or other sexual behavior, to bedwetting or other regressive behavior—with no obvious explanation. The mother may not suspect that her child is being molested by her husband, neighbor, or another person until the painful moment that the evidence is presented.

Julia wasn't able to make sense of her adolescent son's behavior until she learned that her second husband had been molesting him for the past two years. She then agonized through the memories of son and husband eyeing each other across a room and spending long hours together in the boy's room before bedtime. The same trust and love for them that had allowed her to transcend suspicion of these events later made the knowledge of incest almost unbearable.

Catherine believed her 10-year-old physically disabled daughter had grown depressed because she was approaching adolescence and could not join in other children's social activities. She did not know that the child's physical therapist was sexually abusing the girl twice a week until a school nurse told her. Catherine then understood why the girl was upset after many physical therapy sessions.

Mary's 12-year-old daughter Vivian became increasingly involved in their church's youth activities. When the daughter was invited to take trips out of town with the minister and his family, at first Mary approved.

When the Vivian's fixation on the minister became more overt, Mary became suspicious and told her daughter she could not go anymore. Vivian rebelled against her mother's authority and threatened to run away. Believing that the minister's interest in her daughter was inappropriate, Mary followed Vivian to a secret meeting with the man after a church event. There Mary saw and heard exchanges between the two that revealed the man had been sexually abusing Vivian. In retrospect, Mary realized that the minister had begun to be overly critical of her (Mary) nearly a full year before. This had helped him to lessen Vivian's respect for her mother while elevating his own importance in Vivian's life. Mary also remembered other clues. These were later helpful to prosecutors in preparing their legal case.

Children are the primary victims of child sexual abuse, but mothers are the secondary victims. Mothers are faced with the pain of knowing their children have been harmed and then having to find ways of helping and nurturing them through the ordeal. In the meantime, their own traumas are unattended. Two decades of women's groups' efforts to put sexual abuse issues on the public agenda and to establish supportive networks have greatly improved the services where mothers can seek help. But social attitudes, understanding and support are by no means complete.

The difficulty that I had in finding a publisher for the first edition of *The Mother's Book* was one demonstration of low social concern for mothers whose children are abused. On the other hand, the book's sustained success among ever-broader audiences through the years is a measure of increased public recognition of mothers' predicament. Publishers typically think in terms of markets and profits instead of a manuscript's social value, unfortunately. When the original manuscript was completed in late 1984, every publisher I contacted generally thought the book had little or no market value. This included a Seattle-based women's press. Since I had just spent the previous five years working in a Washington state women's shelter and rape crisis center, where the mothers of child victims often asked for "something to read," I knew the book was needed. In fact, I sensed that we were just seeing the proverbial tip of the iceberg in terms of potential audiences for such a book. At a friend's suggestion, I contacted Kendall/Hunt Publishing Company's Seattle representative, Mariel Damaskin. Damaskin recognized the emerging market for sexual assault information written for a specific audience, and, at a personal level, she believed these books should be available. She had earlier been instrumental in publishing other books on sexual assault that had been written by various Seattle area women's organizations. At any rate, I have her and Kendall/Hunt to thank for the existence of *The Mother's Book*. In the early 1990s, on Damaskin's recommendation, Kendall/Hunt also brought Sandi Ashley's manuscript, *The Missing Voice: Writings by Mothers of Incest Victims* (1992), into print. The two books serve as companion volumes and remain two of still very few resources available on the topic.

As I've said, the idea for this mother's survival guide came from mothers themselves. First there was Ellen, who sat beside me for two hours on a Saturday morning in 1979, talking about her daughter's four-year molestation by a family member. Ellen was determined to survive her child's ordeal, thinking she could do more to help her daughter recover if she were strong herself. Ellen's challenges were many, in that her daughter's emotional problems were extensive and the family was having financial and health problems. She left asking if there was something I could recommend for her to read that would prepare her for what lay ahead. At the time, I had only a brochure on child sexual abuse—nothing for moms specifically.

Not long afterward, a personal friend whom I shall call Cory called to say that her adolescent daughter Vickie had been sexually abused by her husband (Vickie's biological father) for more than two years. She had reported the situation, and her daughter had given her statement to investigators. "Now what?" Cory asked. "I feel like I'm falling apart. Is there anything I can read to help me get through the next six months?" The clinical books that touched on the dynamics of incestuous families were few then, and none of these had much breadth and depth in revealing the mother's own experience. The logical place to go for this information was the emerging group of mothers whose kids were reporting abuse in ever growing numbers.

Because I am trained as a researcher and reporter, collecting personal accounts and other material and then writing about them have come as second nature to me. When I left a career in journalism and public information in the late 1970s to work full-time as the administrative director for a women's shelter and rape crisis program in Olympia, Washington, I spent a significant portion of my time in media relations and in producing public education materials—activities to develop better public understanding of sexual assault and domestic violence from the perspectives of those who were most affected by them: victims and survivors. I left the agency in the mid-1980s, setting aside several months to research and write the first edition of *The Mother's Book* before I began graduate school. The project was a gratifying transition for me personally and professionally, because I was helping a large but invisible group of women to speak publicly about their lives. It would take me another decade to understand that *The Mother's Book* was also about my own life.

Few families escape the problems of domestic and sexual violence. As it turned out, my own was no exception. My large extended family was also typical in that we never talked about family violence and sexual assault as things that happened to us, even though the clues were all about. These last years have sent me on a difficult journey to try and open Pandora's box. Finding elders willing to talk has been nearly impossible. It is the members of my own generation within a geographically and emotionally separated family who have begun to speak the truth. The most tragic example of a whistle-blower was my brother Robert, who finally began to provide fragments of his own childhood sexual abuse a few years before his death from drugs and alcohol in 1995. The abuse by an adult female who tormented him all of his 48 years was seen by those he lived with in dreams that made him scream out in the middle of the night, that made him depressed and angry when he was awake, and that sometimes found him verbally and physically abusive. In grieving his painful life and death, I have also been able to remember and better understand our shared childhood and how what was happening to him also affected me. As I gain more information and am able to make sense of it emotionally, I am closer to writing a fuller, more personal account. In the meantime, I begin this revision feeling very much a part of the stories and issues contained in the pages to come.

Most of us survive the traumas in our lives—our own and those of our loved ones. Women whose children are molested survive and move on, even though scars remain. I have seen the mothers I've known through the years respond to this complex, difficult experience in their own remarkable ways, and, in the process, to come into their own personal strength. The term "mother survivor" is an appropriate one for every woman who comes through the trauma of her child's abuse intact. As mother survivors begin to speak more openly about their difficulties, coping mechanisms and insights, we will all learn more about the reality of child sexual abuse. This, in turn, will hopefully empower us to begin to change the society that still allows it to happen.

There is an old Cheyenne saying, "A nation is not conquered until the hearts of its women are on the ground. Then it is done, no matter how strong the weapons, or how brave the warriors." How do all of us as women ensure that our hearts do not hit the ground? What strategies might we as women use to remind us to hold our heads and hearts high?

Ines Hernandez-Avila
poet and professor of
Native American Studies
University of California–Davis*

* Ines Hernandez-Avila, "In Praise of Insubordination," in E. Buchwald, P.R. Fletcher, and M. Roth, *Transforming a Rape Culture*. Minneapolis, MN: Milkweed Editions, 1993, p. 390.

1.

Facts

Facts are easier to come by these days than they were in the 1970s when child molestation and other forms of sexual abuse emerged as modern social concerns. We now have two decades of academic and clinical research, legal data, and published personal accounts of abuse describing the problems in their many aspects. This chapter draws from this body of information to provide current information about child molestation, both that which occurs within the family (incest) and that which occurs outside the family (nonfamilial child molestation).

DEFINITION OF CHILD MOLESTATION

This book uses the terms *child molestation, child sexual abuse,* and *child sexual assault* interchangeably. They are all general terms that refer to a variety of sexual acts committed against children by adults, adolescents, or even other children. Those acts may include either physical or nonphysical sexual interactions with the child. *Physical sexual acts* are those such as fondling of the child's genitals, anus, or breasts; oral-genital acts; or penetration of the vagina, anus, or mouth by a penis (or sometimes another object). *Nonphysical acts* may include voyeurism (watching a child undress or bathe, for instance, for the purpose of achieving erotic pleasure), showing a child pornographic photos, talking in sexually explicit erotic language to the child, or exhibitionism (showing one's genitals to a child). The law is primarily concerned with physically overt acts, as well as exhibitionism, which is also against the law.

However, those of us concerned about understanding the effects of and preventing child sexual abuse should be aware that all of these behaviors are serious and potentially injurious. A school counselor who saw many sexually abused children told the story of a 12-year-old girl who had a nervous breakdown after her stepfather repeatedly told her what he would like to do with her sexually. "He never laid a hand on the girl," the counselor noted, "but that girl was as damaged as many children I've seen who have been physically molested." Offenders often use combinations of these behaviors against children they abuse.

Offenders sometimes say that their activities with children were *consensual*—the child agreed to the sex. Even sexual activity that appears to be conducted with a child's consent is wrong and harmful. Similarly, sex with a child enacted in a seemingly gentle, non-forced manner is abusive. Children, especially very young ones, may not understand or resist the sexual acts by adults. This is typically the case with molestation that begins gradually and continues over time—the child may be gently coached, or *groomed*, to take an active part in the sexual acts. Other children remain passive while the sexual act is occurring. All such activity betrays a child's basic innocence and trust, often by those on whom the child is dependent for nurturance and support. Such sexual activity interferes with children's normal psychological and sexual development by presenting them with feelings and sensations beyond the scope of their developmental abilities to understand and make responsible decisions about the sex.

The effects of the abuse are compounded when the child is made to *keep the secret* that sex has occurred (or continues to go on). The offender may obtain the child's compliance with special gifts and privileges or through threats of harm (physical or other). Either way, the child is emotionally burdened in a way that is both unfair and psychologically overwhelming.

SEXUAL ABUSE AS A SOCIAL ISSUE

The issue has reemerged at different times. Sexual abuse seemed to be a "new problem" when it emerged on the scene in the early 1970s. In fact, the sexual violation of children is a very old, cross-cultural problem that goes on everywhere.

Women, who have been the primary victims of sexual abuse (and other forms of sexual and physical assault by intimates), had begun to speak out about the problem more than a century ago. In our own country, this occurred in the mid- to late-1800s through a social movement to protect children from battering and sexual assault by drunk fathers. One aspect of this movement was the mobilization of public support for a Constitutional amendment to outlaw alcohol (prohibition). These reformers also recognized and tried to protect mothers who were being battered by the same men who abused their children.

The remobilized women's movement (feminism) of the 1960s in the U.S. brought child sexual abuse more clearly into focus and social consciousness. This occurred by way of large numbers of adult women revealing publicly through "speak-outs" that they had been the victims of childhood sexual abuse and other abuse by men. Seeing the magnitude of the problem, feminists offered a new analysis of sexual and physical violence. These, they said, were the result of a social system that allowed men to have greater status and resources than women. Men maintained their status and authority in part through sexual and physical assaults against women (and, by extension, children who were also powerless as a group). This analysis gave women the motivation they needed to try and change values, beliefs, behaviors, policies, and laws that they believed allowed men to abuse women and children.

Increased reporting. Rape crisis programs and battered women's shelters sprang up in small and large communities beginning in 1972. These programs kept a 24-hour crisis line and mostly volunteer staffs to support sexual assault victims and to lead community education and prevention programs. Preventative education was particularly concerned with children, encouraging them to say "NO" if someone tried to touch them in their private parts and to "tell someone" if they were being sexually touched. These prevention programs in public schools and with children's groups, together with increased media attention to the issues, vastly increased reporting of sex crimes against children and adolescents. By the late 1970s, police and child protective service agencies were receiving more calls about incest and molestation than they could manage. The number of calls these agencies received plunged many into crisis— they simply didn't have enough staff to respond.

The lack of staff was often compounded by the lack of training— police academies and social work programs in colleges had not yet begun to educate their professionals about causes of and solutions to child victimization, let alone teach them how to work effectively with sexual abuse victims and families. Increased funding for child protective service staffs, better professional training for these and other personnel, and the creation of procedures for keeping records relating to victims have been some of the outcomes of women's efforts to address child sexual abuse.

The push for prosecution and treatment. Women's organizations all across the country also successfully lobbied for new laws to better enable the investigation and prosecution of those who committed rape, child sexual assault, and battering (family violence). Police were now on the hot seat to investigate crimes they used to seldom see and sometimes chose to ignore; victims' advocates also demanded they be more sensitive to victims, particularly children. Prosecutors, similarly, were pushed to file charges and prosecute alleged offenders for crimes that used to be committed in private, without legal intervention. (Chapter 4 provides a more complete summary of these legal developments.)

Similarly, victims and advocacy groups believed that jail and prison were ineffective to stop sex offenders, who reoffended after they were released. They pushed for treatment programs that focused on the offender accepting responsibility for what he had done, and on learning about the impact of his behavior on victims. With child sex offenders, the mandated treatment (in lieu of incarceration) was intently monitored by courts, and offenders had lengthy parole times afterward. Some programs for incest offenders included a holistic approach, involving other family members in individual and group sessions. This enabled some families to remain together, only with substantially changed guidelines and boundaries for interaction. These programs have had varying degrees of success, and some question their effectiveness. Programs in which ex-offenders become involved as facilitators or therapists have been the most seriously criticized.

There has been surprisingly little public opposition to these developments led by feminists. Even during the conservative years of the 1980s and early 1990s, when feminism was under attack and conservative groups tried to reverse many legal gains of the women's movement, child sexual abuse continued to advance as a major, legitimate social concern. The media, particularly, have increasingly incorporated facts and stories concerned with child sexual abuse into standard news and entertainment formats. Though some published stories and broadcast programs have sensationalized true (or fictionalized) stories or fallen back onto myths of the seductive child (who is made to seem responsible for her own abuse), many adopt the terms, definitions, and analyses of the social movement that has tried to reverse the incidence of child sexual abuse for more than 20 years.

In addition, women's organizations around the world have succeeded in placing sexual and physical violence against women and children on the United Nations' agenda for human rights. This increases the likelihood that the citizens and governments of all nations will find ways of reducing the causes of these crimes.

STATISTICS ON CHILD SEXUAL ABUSE

Sex acts against children are still underreported, both in public records and in independent research. Public records at police agencies, for instance, are estimated to reflect only about 1 in 10 of the crimes actually committed against adult victims and fewer for young victims. Underreporting is the result of victims' mistrust of the criminal justice system (with poor and ethnic minority families especially worried they will be ignored or treated more harshly), fear of the unknown outcome, and shame of telling someone the abuse has happened. Young victims are even less likely than adults to report sexual crimes, especially when the offender is not a stranger. Federal statistics for 1992 (the most recent available) show that about 1 in 4 rape victims in that year were between the ages of 10 and 15, and that about 1 in 3 victims were between 15 and 18. (Figures differ slightly from state to state.)

Victimization studies show that anywhere from 12 to 38 percent of all women, and from 13 to 16 percent of all men are subjected to some form of sexual abuse in their childhood. An estimated 50-90 percent of these are molested within the family. That makes incest the major form of child sexual molestation.

Both federal and independent academic researchers trying to assess the true incidence of child sexual assaults are thwarted. They agree that this population cannot be reliably interviewed. Among the problems that researchers face are that children do not organize their thoughts the same way that adults do. They have limited understanding of the problems they are being asked to speak about (even if they have experienced them). They sometimes give partial answers, and they have limited trust of strangers asking them the questions. And they have short attention spans when researchers need blocks of time as long as an hour or more. Ethical concerns arise over exposing children to questioning of a sexual nature when such questioning may have long-lasting developmental impacts on them.

Based on what we know, we are accurate in saying that child sexual abuse happens a lot and that most of it occurs between members of a household who are likely to be related by marriage. Teens over the age of 15 are statistically more likely to experience their sexual assaults from offenders outside their families, often on dates.

PROFILE OF OFFENDERS

The vast majority of child sex offenders are adult heterosexual males. However, about 1 in 5 incidents of male child victimization is believed to be committed by adult females. In addition, male offenders who specifically abuse adolescent males are likely to have a homosexual sexual orientation. Child sexual offenders come from all walks of life and belong to all racial, ethnic, and religious communities. They range in age from teenagers to elderly men—about half of all child sex offenders apprehended say they began molesting children in their teens.

"Child sex offenders" is a general term that refers to all perpetrators who sexually abuse persons under 16. These perpetrators may also be called by other terms, depending on their crimes. Child molesters, or pedophiles, prey on children younger than 12. Rapists, exhibitionists and peepers are called by the crimes that they commit. Incest offenders are those who prey specifically on children in their own immediate or extended families. Some child sex offenders abuse children both within and outside their families.

Contributing factors. Varied factors contribute to the making of child sex offenders. Many were either battered or sexually abused as children. Most suffer from low self-esteem and underdeveloped senses of self. They may be antisocial and not able to form meaningful adult friendships and love relationships. Some are physically violent toward their victims and others around them. Child sex offenders may be motivated to commit their acts by a sexual attraction to children. They may also be aroused sexually through the act of forcing (or coercing) someone less powerful than themselves to commit a sexual act. They may also believe that someone closer to their own age will not find them appealing—children are perceived as more vulnerable and therefore more available. Others are reenacting the abuse they may have experienced themselves as children as a kind of revenge. All of these motivations demonstrate psychological disturbance. Sex offenders are not exhibiting healthy sexual patterns with persons similar in age and with whom they can enjoy mutually gratifying relations.

All child sex offenders continue to reoffend until they are caught. Most abuse hundreds of children before they die. Stories about the "dirty old man" in the neighborhood or the family is really a way of identifying child molesters. Some offenders reoffend, even after psychological treatment under supervision of the criminal justice system. However, it is essential for child sex offenders to be reported to police and for concerned family members and citizens to cooperate in their apprehension.

Female sex offenders. Little is known about female sex offenders, who are rarely reported. Researchers believe that offenses by females are underreported because society perceives females as victims of, rather than the committers of, sex crimes. In addition, such offenses are believed to be mainly incestuous abuse, which is less often reported than extrafamilial abuse. Females in our society are also given permission to touch children intimately through acts of mothering and other caretaking; therefore, victims may be confused about when and whether they have been sexually exploited.

Studies of reported incidence, as well as published clinical reports, all dating from the 1970s, indicate that mothers mainly molest their sons, though some molest both sons and daughters. In most cases, the husband is absent and the mother may manipulate the son into a pseudo-adult male role in the family. This makes her sexual approaches to him seem more explainable. Mothers are also sometimes involved along with the father (or stepfather) in molesting children in the family. However, women may also molest children outside the family, with the contributing factors being similar to those of male offenders: low self-esteem to seek sex partners of equal status, reenactment of their own early abuse, powerlessness and vulnerability of the child, and so forth. Children abused by women are just as harmed as those molested by males. In fact, the long-term effects may be even more serious in that the abuse may be less likely to be understood and reported by the child.

Offender defense mechanisms. Child sex offenders develop sophisticated if faulty reasoning systems that defend themselves from accepting responsibility for their acts. They minimize the injuries they are inflicting on their young victims, telling themselves this does not harm children (indeed, they may even believe it helps children some way). They also rationalize their acts, convincing themselves that the children seduced them. This keeps them from accepting responsibility for what they do and shifts that blame to the children they abuse. Some also say they are "teaching" the child. Child sex offenders also have powerful denial systems that allow them to say "No, I never did this" when they are questioned. Some offenders' denial systems are so successful that even after months of mandated therapy they continue to say they did nothing wrong.

Although pedophilia is illegal, well-funded organizations like the Man-Boy Love Society continue to advocate for a "child's right" to have "consensual sex" under the age of consent (which is 16 in most states). Concerned citizens should be very wary of the reasoning offered by such groups. Similarly, they should contest efforts within state legislatures to lower the age of sexual consent.

Patterns in offender behavior. Offenders may be society's hated criminals, but they are not always monsters face-to-face. Child sex offenders are able to succeed in molesting so many children through the years, in part, because they are often mild-mannered, likable, and have a way with children. Sex offenders in the family are especially adept at manipulation—they orchestrate when people go and come, they create elaborate pretenses for being alone with the child and having no one suspect, and they are masters at explaining and excusing their behavior to the child victim. Incestuous pedophiles typically begin grooming the child early in her or his life by touching the child in increasingly sexual ways—during baths, while teaching about body parts, playing doctor, etc. All pedophiles develop interests, even occupations, that allow them to be in close proximity with children on a frequent basis. Therefore, once caught, even treated, doesn't mean the game is over. Divorced pedophiles marry again—especially to women with children the age they like to molest. Nonfamilial offenders get right back into their roles as coaches, youth leaders, and other roles or activities that increase their regular, legitimate encounters with children. Therapists agree there is no cure for child sex offenders. Therefore, strict measures are needed to control and monitor them.

IMPACT ON VICTIMS

Children who have been sexually abused respond in a variety of ways, depending on the length and frequency of the abuse, their relationship to the offender, their age and psychological makeup, their perception of what has happened to them, and the ways that others respond to them when they disclose the abuse.

Children who have been taught to tell someone about sexual touching or other behavior that makes them uncomfortable are the most likely to get help and protection the quickest. Thus, the necessary intervention to stop the abuse and afford the child with necessary emotional support (and, hopefully, the offender with arrest) can be enormously therapeutic for that child. Children who are molested even once and tell no one carry this terrible secret around them; this can result in long-term feelings of worthlessness, cause fearfulness of further abuse, and generate various behavioral problems.

Children who experience repeated abuse by someone close to them, in the family or outside the family, stand the greatest chance of damage to normal psychological and sexual development. They feel deeply ashamed, afraid, and worthless. Some feel extreme rage but may internalize this until it erupts as antisocial behavior or is turned against themselves. These children are at risk of developing learning disabilities, regressive behavior, eating and sleeping disorders, rebellious acting out in the form of running away, truancy, alcohol and drug abuse, and even assaultive behavior toward other children. The most severely damaged children may have difficulty making friends and trusting, loving relationships. They may live in a make-believe world detached from reality, and some may develop multiple personalities. Self-destruction (burning or cutting) may also be present.

Children of any age may develop sexually transmitted diseases through sexual activity.

SOCIAL CONTEXT FOR ABUSE

Child molesters are given tacit approval by society to use children for sexual gratification when nothing definitive is done to identify and stop them.

Silence has been a powerful agent in perpetuating incest and other child molestation. The silence of victims has been reinforced by the stigma of sexual molestation, which has fallen primarily on the victims who have been allowed to feel ashamed and guilty for what has happened to them. Society has not, until recently, begun to direct responsibility more appropriately on offenders and to treat victims as the innocent parties.

Silence has also been encouraged by social tendencies to minimize the offender's behavior. Jokes about "dirty old men," may really been about the uncle or grandfather who couldn't keep his hands off the children, the neighborhood joker who cornered young girls for kisses, or the kindly old fool who liked to hold kids on his lap and tickle them senseless. Older females who were molested by these dirty old men knew to keep their own children away from them, but they may never have spoken out or reported them. Similarly, jokes about "the farmer's daughter" minimize men's lust for vulnerable adolescent girls and they present those girls as seductresses and willing whores. Humor lets offenders off the hook, tells victims that their pain doesn't matter, and absolves others who know but don't tell from assuming responsibility. There has been entirely too much laughing about child molestation for the good of victims and their families.

Child molestation also continues because of inadequate laws and a legal system that still varies in its willingness to prosecute and punish (or treat) offenders. Molestation also occurs because we condition children to obey adult authority. Unless a child has had prior encouragement to resist others' demands for sex, or to report it to adults who can help them when it does occur, they may be unprepared to protect themselves.

Lastly, women's inequality contributes to a society in which one gender has substantially more authority and control over the other. Women must gain fuller educational, personal, and socioeconomic status, on a par with men's, so they will be able to stand up for themselves and their children—the primary targets of sex abuse.

References

"Adult Sexual Assault," *Journal of Social Issues* (special issue), Vol. 48, No. 1, 1992.

Gordon, Linda. (1988). *Heroes of their Own Lives: The Politics and History of Domestic Violence*. New York: Penguin Books.

Hunter, Mic. (1990). *Abused Boys: The Neglected Victims of Sexual Abuse*. Lexington, MA: Lexington Books.

Mayer, Adele. (1992). *Women Sex Offenders*. Holmes Beach, FL: Learning Publications, Inc.

Sexual Assault Information About Offenders (booklet). (no date). Seattle, WA: Harborview Sexual Assault Center.

Strong, Marilee. (1997). "Monsters in Our Midst," World Wide Web (*http://www.diablopubs.com/focus/ARCHIVES/FEATURES/sexoffenders.html*).

When the Victim is a Child (second edition). National Institute of Justice, U.S. Department of Justice, March 1992.

2.

Disclosure

Mothers usually say that learning about their child's sexual abuse was the most difficult moment of their lives. You may have learned about your child's molestation when the child told you herself or himself, or when a child protective services worker arrived on your doorstep, or when the school principal called you to come in and meet with her or him. Whether it was these or another way, you will never forget it or how you felt. This chapter explores mothers feelings immediately following the disclosure of their child's abuse, and it provides some options for surviving it.

MOTHER'S FEELINGS

Mothers report a wide range of emotional responses to their children's disclosure of sexual abuse. Responses vary according to the number of other crises present in a mother's life, her experiences handling crises under other circumstances, whether or not she was a victim of abuse herself, the nature of her relationship to the child and the offender, her level of self-esteem and self-confidence to manage new situations, her knowledge of sexual abuse and where to go for help, her religious and cultural teachings about sexuality and abuse, her values and belief system, her personal support system, and so forth. There is no "most appropriate" way of feeling or responding.

The following stories illustrate the way that several women learned about their children's abuse and how they responded emotionally.

Story #1: SHARON

Sharon's 15-year-old daughter Angie told her on a Friday afternoon. It was an angry disclosure following a disagreement between the two over how late that night Angie should stay out on a date. "What do you think we're going to do—have sex?" Angie asked her mother when Sharon questioned her about why she and her boyfriend couldn't be back by midnight. Before Sharon could answer, Angie added resentfully, "Well, it wouldn't be the first time anyway. And, Chip wouldn't be the first!"

Sharon asked Angie what she was talking about, and the girl revealed that her father had been having sex with her for two years. "And what are you going to do about that?" she yelled and ran out of the house.

Remembering back, Sharon described her initial reaction to Angie's disclosure as one of numbness and distance:

> I felt like I was in the middle of a slow-motion movie. I wondered if I was watching this happen to someone else. What Angie was telling me seemed incredible. Was she lying, I asked myself? At first, I thought I should stay calm and figure this out. Since I couldn't feel anything anyway, staying calm wasn't really a problem. Then I thought maybe I shouldn't stay calm! I should do something! Yet I wasn't sure what to do. So, I sat down after Angie ran out of the house and tried to think back. As the last few years passed before me, I realized all the clues were there. Only I hadn't understood them. I realized that it had begun while I was working on the school board election one summer and Evan was taking care of the girls. Everyone began to act differently that summer, but I just thought the girls were just growing up and family tensions were part of that. Now I knew that Angie had to be telling the truth. I waited until the next day when we could be alone and talked with her again. I told her that I believed her. We made a plan for what we would do, which started by going to the Sheriff. Angie had known for two years that what was happening was wrong—even illegal—but she wouldn't talk about it. She said that she thought I must already know. I was devastated by that.

Story #2: ANA

Ana learned about her daughter Maria's abuse from a child protective service caseworker. It seemed that 7-year-old Maria told her teacher and principal about the abuse after they began to suspect the problem. Maria's teacher had watched the child change behavior over a period of weeks. Usually a cheerful little girl who liked school, Maria would grow quiet and withdrawn now on some mornings. She had taken to drawing her coat around her and refusing to take it off. Some days she would be the last to leave the bus, because she didn't want to go home. Her teacher conferred with the principal about Maria's strange behavior, and together they talked to Maria. Maria said that her stepfather made her do things that hurt and scared her. The teacher and principal called child protective services, and after recording their statements, the caseworker went to Ana's place of work.

Ana remembers reacting angrily toward the caseworker who was accusing her new husband, Arturio, of molesting her daughter:

I yelled at her—she came here to accuse my husband and break up our family! What did she know? Then I realized what she was saying—I was so mad at him! How could he do this to Maria? And then I was mad at Maria—why didn't she tell me? I would have stopped it. I guess I was mad at everybody around me. I tried to calm down so everyone wouldn't hear us talking [in the employees' lunch room]. I didn't want them to know.

Later, I just sat down and thought about what this really meant, and I felt scared. In a few hours he could be in jail. And, even if they didn't arrest him, I could never bring myself to be with him again. The children and I could starve. I didn't make enough money for us to live on. I didn't have anyone to take care of the kids when I was working. What were we going to do?

Ana's family was also faced with a legal problem—Arturio was an illegal immigrant from Mexico who had been in the U.S. only a year. In the midst of the disclosure trauma, Ana feared having to be involved with people at the U.S. Immigration and Naturalization Service.

Story #3: MELANIE

Melanie thought it odd that Justin, 4, was rubbing his bottom one evening. "Do you have an itch?" she remembers asking him. "No, it hurts," Justin told her. She asked if he had hurt himself or anything else was wrong, and he answered angrily, "No!" Thinking her child might have a rash that needed treating, Melanie eventually inspected the child and found excessive redness around his anus. Melanie worked to stay calm and talk to Justin in a quiet voice about his problem. Justin explained that the 14-year-old boy from down the block, who had baby-sat for him on several occasions, had taken Justin up to play in the treehouse earlier that afternoon. The boy had made Justin promise not to tell, adding that "Nobody will believe you anyway." Melanie assured Justin that she believed him and that this wouldn't happen again.

> I felt incredibly guilty—I let this happen to Justin. And sad. I wanted to cry. But I needed to seem strong and together for Justin. I wanted to comfort him, to make this go away, to make him feel okay again. When I saw the damage the boy had done to my son, I felt a deep loss for him. His childhood innocence was gone. Why had I left Justin with this kid—I hardly even knew him! Somehow I felt responsible. Later, after talking to the rape crisis advocate, I realized that I still felt the grief and sadness over my own sexual abuse. When I was 6, an older cousin had raped me on a family picnic. He told me he'd kill me if I ever told anyone. So I never had. The cousin raped me two more times before his parents moved to another city. My childhood seemed to end after I was abused. Would Justin's childhood be over too, I wondered?

EMOTIONAL RESPONSES VARY

As these stories illustrate, mothers respond in a variety of ways after learning about their children's sexual abuse. It's important to point out that there is no "most appropriate" or "typical" way to feel in the midst of this trauma.

Mothers often describe an inability to experience any emotion or physical sensation when they are told their child has been molested. They use the word *numbness*. Some women also say they seemed to be "in shock." Mothers also describe feeling distant, or separated from the people and events around them during the initial moments. This reaction may be a way of stepping back and looking at the situation. It buys time before you have to respond to the difficult demands in front of you. This stage of initial trauma lasts a few minutes to a few hours—until the reality of what has happened sets in.

When feelings do return, many mothers *feel angry* at everyone around them, a kind of general anger. Others experience anger at someone in particular, the abused child or the offender often heading the list. It may seem natural to be angry with the child, with whom you may have had a troubled relationship or whom you have felt pulling away from you. The mother-daughter bond is particularly damaged in the case of incest, and mothers not infrequently blame their daughters and feel hostile toward them.

Some mothers get angry at the messenger, the person who came and told them about the abuse—the police officer, child protective worker, preschool teacher. It's also very common for mothers to feel angry at themselves for all sorts of things—not recognizing the signs of abuse, not protecting the child better, not being a better mother. In a society that blames moms for far too much anyway, mothers too often easily take on all the responsibility for what has happened.

The person you are really angry at, of course, is the offender. This may be harder to acknowledge, for a variety of reasons. If this person is your partner or husband, you may have trusted him and have trouble accepting what he has done. Or you may fear him—his power, his abuse toward you and your children, etc. If the offender is a stranger, you may have trouble conjuring up anger at an unknown person. However, anger can be a healthy response to what has happened when directed at the person who is really to blame. By directing your anger appropriately, you can keep the facts in better perspective and make decisions to best benefit yourself and your child(ren).

Hatred, brought on by extreme anger, is something that many women feel toward the offender. Feelings of hatred sometimes lead to fantasies of hurting the person who has harmed your child. One mother said that she alternately fantasized "reaching my hands around his throat and choking him" and "hitting his face as hard as I could." Another dreamed of hearing a jury pronounce him "guilty" and seeing him led off to prison. Another wished he would get a fatal disease and die. The old adage, "be careful of what you wish, because it may come true," comes to mind in the case of the mother whose ex-husband died of cancer before she could have him prosecuted for molesting her two children for many years. She is now trying to resolve her hatred toward the man through therapy. Most women are able to direct their hatred and anger in healthy ways that are both socially acceptable and, in the long run, the most positive for themselves and their children. A desire for revenge, for instance, may best be achieved by letting the criminal justice system do your dirty work.

In the initial stages, there may be frequent moments of *disbelief*. Is this real? Am I dreaming? Has this really happened to my child and me? What helps the disbelief to go away is usually more information about the abuse—how and when it happened, what the nature of the abuse included, etc.

You may be inclined to *minimize the seriousness* of what has happened, telling yourself that "She (or he) will be okay—this won't really be a big deal." Or, you may say, "This only happened once—he's told me he won't do it again, and I believe him." Or, you may not believe your child has told the truth at all, especially if the offender continues to deny that he has done anything wrong. You may even resist accepting evidence when it is presented to you. Minimizing and denying are ways that we protect ourselves from emotional pain. Since children rarely lie about sexual abuse, you will want to explore the information at hand carefully and accept its veracity. You cannot really be supportive to your child until you have moved through the denial stage. Neither can you do the things for yourself to become strong in the face of increased responsibility these next days and weeks.

Mothers frequently report feeling *insignificant and invisible* after their children are abused. All the attention is suddenly focused on your child and (if in the family) the offender. Your feelings and needs may seem secondary to everyone else, especially if you believe your role as a mother is to help others and put your own needs aside. You may be in a room full of people, but no one is paying attention to you, and this situation may repeat itself over and over again. The events swirl around you but seemingly don't involve you. If this is happening to you, stop and pay attention. Ask yourself what you need from others and how you can get this. Try to identify moments outside the required activities with police and others when you can seek your own peace of mind and support from someone—a friend, a trusted relative, a rape crisis counselor, a minister, etc.

Guilt and self-blame are closely associated with self-directed anger. These feelings are strongest in mothers whose children tried to tell them about the abuse, and, for whatever reason, mothers didn't believe their children or were otherwise unable to stop the abuse from happening again. While there may be reason to examine your own role in the problem you are now confronted with, and to develop better skills at protecting your child, it's also important to keep your perspective about who is responsible for what has happened. This is the offender who has committed the abuse and has sole blame. Remind yourself of this often. Also, work on being assertive so that you can stand up for yourself and your child when others try to point fingers at you.

Feelings of *shame* are companions to guilt and blame, and are worst in families where incest has been going on over a period of time. These feelings are also most deeply experienced by mothers who still have not resolved their own childhood sexual abuse. Feeling ashamed for what has happened may be a response to what you believe others are thinking of you and your family. You may also feel personal shame for having loved and been intimate with a man who was having sexual relations with your child. Shame also arises from believing that you have been sinful and your child, perhaps, is being punished for what you have done. Shame is a powerful, important emotion to examine with a counselor who is trained to work with sexual abuse and mothers.

Hurt and betrayal are especially common feelings in mothers whose children were molested by a family member. You put your trust in this person, and now he has betrayed that trust. These emotions are often expressed by mothers whose adolescent daughters have been abused by a husband or boyfriend. In these cases, you have become the outsider, cast aside. The hurt is deep because you know they worked so hard to keep the secret from you, even to scheme against you. They have taken your love and trust for granted and operated in the home environment you considered safe, perhaps even sacred.

Such situations also generate feelings of *jealousy* in mothers. Your daughter (or son) has replaced you in your primary sexual relationship, assuming the special place of intimacy you thought was yours. One mother, whose daughter was molested from the age of 7 until she was 14, by her second husband, said that each time she felt jealous toward her teenage daughter, she took out the photo of her daughter at the age when the abuse began to remind herself that it was this small, vulnerable child who fell prey to the husband's assaults. That helped her feel less jealous and more angry (which she believed was the appropriate emotion).

Incestuous abuse often makes mothers question their own sexual attractiveness and adequacy. You may also feel *rejected* by the offender whom you believe preferred your child to yourself. If you have these feelings of inadequacy and rejection, remind yourself that it is a psychologically disturbed man who prefers sexual gratification from a child rather than an adult woman. Your sexual qualities were not a factor in his irresponsible, unhealthy behavior.

Mothers not uncommonly report feeling *protective* toward the offender, whether a family member or someone outside the family. This is especially common when the offender shows remorse for what he has done, or when the offender is a youth. Feeling protective toward the person who has committed the offense may be a maternal feeling but it is one that can be debilitating. One consequence could be that you confuse loyalties—your child or the offender? Examine these feelings carefully and talk to someone about them.

Mothers sometimes feel *repulsion*—both sexual and physical—toward the child's offender. Some women even experience nausea when the offender comes into a room. One mother said, "I felt physically sick when I knew I'd have to see him again." The offender has committed a terrible act, and such a reaction is not unwarranted.

Confronted with the trauma of disclosure, some mothers experience confusion and self-doubt. Common questions include: "Am I doing the right thing (with regard to the many decisions that have to be made)?" "Whom can I trust?" "What if I make the wrong choice?" "What should I do next?" Your judgment is no longer certain, your coping skills may seem unavailable to you, your moment-to-moment behavior may appear to be erratic. Such feelings typically come and go through the initial stages and off and on in the period to follow. Most women report needing others to talk to so they can keep their bearings, check out their perceptions, get encouragement, and brainstorm options for decisions.

PRACTICAL CONSIDERATIONS

Safety for yourself and your children may be a fact of immediate concern to you. If you have been living with your child's offender, and that person has either threatened you or had a habit of abusing you, you may need to seek a women's shelter for safety. Doris, who lived in a rural region, had been battered for several years by her husband. Each time she left him, he found her and brought her back. He often kept a loaded rifle near his chair at home to remind her that she should not "step out of line" with him. The last time he brought her back, he said he would kill her and the kids if they left him again. When Doris learned that her husband was molesting their oldest daughter, age 9, she took the children and fled to a battered women's shelter. From there, she began legal proceedings on the molestation. Her husband was prosecuted and sent to prison, promising as he went that he would get out and "come back" for them all. Doris has a very serious, long-term safety problem to tackle now.

Financial concerns often arise in the cases where mothers are economically reliant on the child's offender. If you separate or divorce your partner, if he loses his job over the allegations, or if he is sent to jail or prison, you may be confronted with a significant or total loss of income. This issue is serious and real for many women, but it is also one that can be addressed. You may be tempted to avoid reporting the child's abuse because you fear you will not be able to support your children without him. If this is the case, you will want to get the emotional support of a rape crisis counselor who can see you through the tough early stage, to stick by you as you think through your economic options, and to make referrals so you can get employment counseling and training.

Lifestyle changes are often unavoidable. Child sexual abuse interferes with your life—and the lives of others in the family—in ways that sometimes bring irreversible changes. Sometimes these life changes are foisted on mothers by circumstance; other times, they come about as a result of plans and choices. Changes begin as early as the disclosure stage for many women, but other times, these evolve with the situation. For example:

- Rhonda found herself going to work after being a full-time mother for 10 years. She was overwhelmed at first but managed to find good day care and a job that paid enough for her and the kids to live on.

- Carmen decided to pick up her two kids and move across the country to start over in a new community. Without a judgmental family or reminders of the pain she had endured with her children's abuse around her each day, she found great freedom and hope. She changed their last name and enrolled the children in a school where no one knew them. "We are all doing much better," she reports.

- Mary Margaret, the children's grandmother, brought the girls to live with her and her husband because she realized that neither her son nor their mother (whose new husband had molested the girls) were stable enough to raise the daughters on their own. She and her husband had to give up space and time they had worked years to enjoy. They still see this as a short-term answer to a long-term problem.

- Janeen had to look for a new job, since her former employer was the one who had molested her adolescent daughter. Even though the man was found guilty and sent to jail, he would return. Changing jobs meant leaving behind not just a good income but a social support system she had counted on for years. She then had multiple losses to contend with but felt she had no other choice.

COPING WITH DISCLOSURE

You are entitled to whatever feelings you have when you first learn about your child's sexual abuse, as well as those that arise later on. The important thing is being able to identify your feelings, to be able to interpret them for yourself, and to let your feelings help you make the decisions that must be made. In other words, you will want your feelings to help motivate you rather than to block you. This, of course, is easier said than done sometimes. There is no single best way to accomplish your journey through the tangled emotional web during and following the disclosure.

Mothers who've been through this advise finding someone to talk to as soon as you can—someone you trust. This may or may not be someone you already know (a family member, friend, minister, etc.). You may feel more comfortable with a counselor or advocate from the local sexual assault center or women's shelter (these services typically have 24-hour crisis service). Rape counselor advocates are trained to listen to you, help you make sense of the situation for yourself, accompany you to agencies to report the crime or seek other service, and make referrals to other services. Moms with supportive families or personal networks already in place can also rely on these for survival.

FIRST STEPS AFTER DISCLOSURE

There are several basic first steps that mothers may want to take after learning the child has been molested.

- *Believe the child*. Young children almost never lie about having been sexually touched. While teens are statistically more likely to fabricate a story of abuse, even they rarely disclose something that didn't happen. Accepting your child's story will help you to cope with your own emotional reactions to the abuse and to make the many decisions about your own and your family's future.

- *Talk with your child*. Tell the child that what has happened is not her or his fault. Assure the child that you will protect her or him and explain how you will try to do this. Reassure the child that it was good that she/he told someone about the abuse. Begin to rebuild any bonds you feel have been damaged by the abuse.

- *Report the abuse to police or child protective services.* What has happened to your child can only be stopped with legal intervention. Even counseling for the offender requires a legal mandate and long-term monitoring. These lie beyond the scope of your legal powers.

- *Be persevering in the face of opposition.* In the rare situation, like Sarah's, in which the criminal justice system did not find her ex-husband guilty of abusing their very young daughter and she is required to allow visitation rights to a man she believes to be still abusing her child, try to explain to the child that you will continue to try stop the problem. Encourage the child to tell you whenever the abuse happens. Keep records so that you can pursue a legal remedy for this.

- *Consider confronting the offender.* Though an optional step, and clearly difficult, some mothers find it empowering to deliver a carefully planned speech to the person who abused their children. Let others help you with this, and anticipate (and find answers to) his denials and rationalizations. Find the appropriate time and place to say what you need to say. Take someone you trust with you.

- *Trust yourself.* You have the wisdom and strength to get through this. In your years as a woman and mother, you have amassed much knowledge and practical experience. Though you may feel like an emotional mess from the trauma your child's sexual abuse has brought into your life, you have the inner resources to get through this crisis.

- *Seek support.* But you don't have to do it all by yourself. You have the right to ask for support and understanding at this very difficult time. Give yourself permission to do this. You will pull through as many others have done.

I am reminded that we do not heal from the past by forgetting it. The dark does not disappear. There is memory. There are aftershocks. And even as the aftereffects unto many generations begin to disappear, there is the dark within us. . . The enemy is not outside us but in us. . . And is this terrifying? Yes, but also thrilling, provoking another kind of courage that gives us more than death.

Susan Griffin
writer and poet*

---

* Susan Griffin, "The Not Yet Spoken," in E. Buchwald, P.R. Fletcher, and M. Roth, *Transforming a Rape Culture*, Minneapolis, MN: Milkweed Editions, 1993, p. 448.

3.

Taking Care of Yourself

Mothers' reactions to their children's molestation are followed by a complex set of needs, some emotional, some practical, all of them personal. Mothers say they get through the ordeal of their children's abuse when they take care of themselves. Like reactions to the disclosure, specific short- and long-term needs vary from woman to woman. The following needs are commonly discussed.

FOLLOWING THE DISCLOSURE

"Someone to talk to" heads the list of what mothers need once they have learned about their children's abuse. They need someone to listen respectfully, to be sympathetic, and to trust to care about their own welfare as mothers. The listener might be a friend, a member of the family (mothers and sisters are high on the list), a minister with knowledge of child molestation, or a rape crisis advocate. Some mothers seek a therapist immediately; others wait. Mothers are especially hoping this (or these) trusted person(s) say, "This wasn't your fault," when they hear mothers talk about their feelings. The need for people to listen tends to be ongoing. Therefore, some mothers recommend having several confidantes to call.

"Someone to counsel me about my own molestation" is also a common need, in the case of mothers who have experienced their own abuse. The child's victimization brings back all the feelings and memories of the mother's own abuse. If you haven't talked to someone about what happened to you, or if you are reexperiencing feelings of trauma even after you thought you'd worked this all out, now is an important time to address this situation. You may not only find it helpful but essential to you if you are going to face the reality of your child's abuse. A rape crisis advocate or a private therapist with training in past sexual assault will be a vital support to you now.

Mothers say that they both fear knowing but need "to know what happened" in the child's abuse. While painful, they need basic facts about the nature and extent of the abuse, the time and places that it happened, and the child's feelings. Women also need to "know I wasn't the only mother this happened to." The isolation that you may experience is overcome by talking about it in general, but also seeking out a mother's group made up of other women like yourself. In the event that no such group exists in your community, consider asking the rape crisis center, battered women's shelter, or mental health clinic to form a group.

In families where incest has occurred, mothers express the need "to have a break from him." In other words, they need a physical separation from the offender in order to gain perspective, consider their feelings about the relationship, and "to break up the game we were caught up in," as one mother put it. Even women who hope to reconcile after the offender has been through treatment need to have him leave the house temporarily. This is usually mandated by the court.

You, like other mothers, will also want "to be treated like a person," to have your feelings listened to seriously, to feel respected, to be acknowledged when you are present, to be cared about and not taken by granted by children, friends, or people in the various legal and helping service systems. If people don't respond to you as you need or want, you may need to gently ask or remind them. Assertiveness counts.

Women have an urgent need "to regain control of my own life and mind." Particularly in cases of incest, mothers express the need to recover a sense of control over day-to-day events, their own thoughts, and their own space. You have had these taken away from you to one degree or another, or you feel that you have, perhaps even without realizing it. You can feel more in charge of yourself and your life if you plan how to take them back and seek support from others to succeed.

Unless you have experience interacting with police, courts, child protective services, therapists, and all the other people who will seemingly invade your life, you may crave "basic information on how to survive the system." Rape crisis centers are a good place to go with your questions and to get handouts to help you navigate through lengthy processes and keep your wherewithal intact.

A woman who has been emotionally or physically abused by the same man who molested her child may have a special need "to understand how my husbands battering of me related to the incest." If this is you, your need for information will be essential, of course, but only a first step toward a longer therapeutic process of examining your abusive relation-ship. Seek help at your local women's shelter program, which can provide printed information, individual support, and mother's groups.

As the preceding chapter discusses at the end, all women need support in order "to make basic life decisions about myself and my child(ren)." Should you move to a new neighborhood or city to avoid public scrutiny? Should you divorce your husband (assuming he was the abuser)? Whom should you tell about what has happened? These are only a few basic questions that arise in the aftermath of your child's abuse.

Mothers with additional children typically want "to know how my abused child and other children will react" to the abused child and the situation this has presented. You will wonder about how to recognize signs of trauma in your child, and how to respond. This is true whether the abuse has been by someone within or outside the family, because everyone is affected by what has happened. There are several ways that you can educate yourself about the abuse and its traumatic effects. You have already taken one step by reading this book. You can also pursue the references at the end of some of the chapters in this book, and at the end of this book in the section "Recommended Reading." Also, talk to a child advocate at your rape crisis center, or to a counselor specializing in abused children and family therapy. You can also take the plunge and begin talking to other mothers you know—chances are one of them has gone through this herself or knows someone else who has. This will begin to tie you into a supportive network to help you address the critical parenting issues.

"To know my rights regarding custody" is uppermost in the minds of mothers whose kids were abused by their husbands. Your child may have been placed in protective custody with a foster family, while the case is under investigation, so the question of parental rights arises immediately. Because laws and procedures vary from state to state, get a legal advocate at a women's shelter or rape crisis center as soon as possible to inform you of what you are about to encounter. Meanwhile, one mother advises to "sign NOTHING" until you are absolutely sure about your rights.

Every mom wants to know how "to make sure this won't happen again." Taking steps to safeguard your child is important. In the case of incest, this usually entails understanding legal ground rules (such as how and when the court will permit contact between child and offender) and guidelines for interaction laid down by the offender's court-appointed therapist. The therapist's guidelines will probably involve an agreement that the offender will not be alone with the child until she or he is 21, and that the contact will not be sexual in any way. All mothers can help to protect their children from future victimization, however, by teaching them assertiveness and encouraging them always to tell you or someone else if someone tries to engage them sexually. Children over the age of 6 can also benefit from taking a self-defense course or training in martial arts. Self-protection will be a life-long process for you and your child.

FACING THE MEMORIES

Once your child has told you about the molestation, you can expect what one mother described as a "flood of memories" to wash over you. You may continue to be haunted by your child's story and trauma for months to come. You will certainly never forget this and what it has done to your life. You will continue to examine your own relationship to the abuse and wonder what, if anything, you could have done to prevent it or, in the case of incest, to have stopped it sooner. While these are natural reflections, they should be put into context through counseling or other supportive interactions so that you can stop feeling responsible for what the offender has done.

Incestuous abuse makes the memories especially consuming. As you piece together the events, and the bigger picture (and your location in it) comes into focus, you should prepare yourself to contend with moments of painful insights. At the least expected time—when you are in a crowd, driving your car, cleaning house, doing other familiar things—new realizations will come to you. Some of these will help you make sense of the situation. Others will be disturbing. Each new realization will bring its own set of emotions for you to grapple with. You may want to scream with rage, as Mary did. She said it helped her to go out into the big field by her house and literally yell at the moon and sky. Sometime she would be overcome with rage when she was alone driving. She learned to pull the car over to the side of the road, turn the radio up full blast and scream as loud as she could. You, too, must find some ways to let the emotions OUT. You may need to put your friends and other support people "on call"—tell them your call could come at any hour and you will need to talk, maybe cry. Also remind yourself that while remembering can be painful, it also enables you to come to terms with the whole truth of your child's molestation and to deal realistically with the facts.

RELATIONSHIP TO THE OFFENDER

Making decisions about how and whether to maintain interaction with a child molester known to your family raises some complicated questions. All sorts of things will enter into the solutions you define for yourself.

Proximity to the offender (if he is a neighbor or someone else your child might run into) can make you feel trapped, threatened, and resentful. If he is a member of your immediate or extended family, you may feel his presence close in around you. You can define the necessary physical distance between the offender and you and your children to make you feel safe and out of his sphere. Also, consider the means you have to enforce this distance: The legal system? The help of friends and family to serve as "guards"? Your own assertive boundary-setting? Your child(ren)?

Emotional attachment is one of the most powerful factors affecting mothers' future relationships to their children's molesters. In the case of a husband or partner, common issues include whether or not you love him, whether or not you feel you can ever trust him again, religious or cultural beliefs about divorce, economic factors (namely whether you can survive without his income), his willingness to undergo counseling and change in behavior, and his feelings for you and your child(ren). If the molester is another one of your children (e.g., the victim's brother or stepbrother), you may feel torn by competing parental urges to nurture and to punish. When the molester is a member of the extended family or friendship circle, you are confronted by how to renegotiate complex patterns of abuse. One critical ground rule in incestuous families, regardless of which family member was the offender, is to put the facts out in the open. Presumably there will have been some form of legal and therapeutic intervention. Creating a new climate of openness, one in which sexual secrets are no longer kept, is one part of the therapeutic process within families. But don't expect to get applause for instigating this. You (and possibly your child) may, instead, be scapegoated and labeled as a troublemaker. In dysfunctional families, the one(s) who gets healthy is not uncommonly targeted and blamed for disrupting the established order. Be ready for these developments when you assess your emotional bonds.

Women whose husbands or partners were the offenders, and who decide to remain in a relationship with the men, face deep personal questions around rebuilding trust, sexual contact, openness, and interaction that is more egalitarian (in terms of respect, shared responsibilities and privileges). Reestablishing sexual relations with someone who has molested your child presents many women with overcoming revulsion toward him. Charlaine said that it was a full year before she could bear to have him touch her, and then it was gradual. Long-term couple counseling is essential if this relationship is to become healthier and work. In the process, remember: You are entitled to have your sexual and emotional needs met within this relationship.

IF YOU ARE A BATTERED WOMAN

Families in which incest occurs also may experience other symptoms of dysfunction. One problem often present, for instance, is domestic violence between the offender and his spouse (you). You are technically a "battered woman" if you experience any of the following:

- *Emotional abuse:* He calls you ugly, fat, slut, bitch, pig, or other insults and put-downs. He tells you no one else will want you if you leave him. He treats you like a child. He humiliates you in front of others. He ignores you and/or withholds affection, especially to punish you for something minor (which he may be making up). He isolates you from your friends and family. He threatens the children with harm, or threatens to commit suicide unless you do what he wants.

- *Physical abuse:* He keeps you at home in such a way that you feel "imprisoned." He holds you down or against a wall to show you he's boss. He pushes or shoves you. He slaps you (open-handed) or punches you (fist), hits you with objects, or throws things at you. He kicks you, uses guns or other weapons to make you afraid or to control you.

- *Sexual abuse:* He calls you degrading sexual names or makes jokes about your body or the way you make love. He criticizes you for not being a good lover. He coerces you to have sex when you don't want to, or he holds you down and makes you submit to sexual acts. (Note: These acts are legally considered rape, even between married persons, in most states.) He tortures you physically during sex. He engages in sexual affairs with other women (either secretly or blatantly). He compares you sexually to other women, especially in the way you make love.

There are additional abuses that cut across more than one of these category, the most important perhaps being the withholding of monetary or other resources. Men who give their wives no access to checking accounts or other resources are behaving abusively.

It is important for you to acknowledge these experiences and to address their effect on your life. Most women's shelters offer a safe haven to you and your children, as well as advocacy, counseling, support groups and referral to other services. In addition, most states now protect wives and partners from domestic abuse through restraining orders, arrest, or other protection.

IF YOUR CHILD VICTIM IS MALE

As discussed in Chapter 1, researchers now believe that as many as 1 in 5 (20%) of child sexual abuse victims may be male. This estimate is borne out to some extent by slowly increasing reports by male victims, and the increased numbers of males seeking crisis and other counseling. Still, this category of victims still greatly underreports their abuse. Why? One reason is a fear on the part of victims that if they were molested by someone of the same sex, this means they (the victims) are homosexual. Reporting the abuse, they reason, will tell the world they are gay. This fear, of course, has no basis in fact. Most offenders choose their victims because of availability. Child and adolescent victims may not yet have well-established sexual identities, so an offender would have no particular way of knowing whether a youth is heterosexual or homosexual.

However, this kind homophobia—a fear of same-sex identity— prevents someone who has been harmed from feeling safe enough to seek help. This is the tragedy, and it is one that we must eradicate if we are going to overcome the conditions that allow child sexual assault to go on. Until social attitudes about homosexuality become more accepting, many children and adolescents will suffer their abuses in silence. This could seriously damage and destroy them.

Another reason that male victimization is not reported is that social norms around masculinity create a context in which abuse against males is still not named such. The sexual activity may be interpreted as a sexual encounter. Or, if with a female outside the family, as sexual initiation. A former university football star confided to the author, for instance, that he had had his first sexual experience when he was 12—with the 35-year-old mother of his best friend, who lived in the next apartment. "Yeah, everybody knew it," he said. "It was a pretty big deal—none of the guys could top that one." In other words, his exploitation by a female was treated like a first sexual conquest by himself and everyone else. He was a grown man before he questioned what had happened.

Males are also supposed to be strong, emotionally in control, and stoic—in other words, "a real man" when something painful happens to them. Young boys conditioned into such a value system believe it to be socially unacceptable to share their abuse experience as such. Closely related to this value is the myth that sexual abuse is less harmful to boys than it is to girls. All the evidence points to nearly identical injurious effects on both sexes (see Chapter 1). This double standard for male and female children is inherently inegalitarian, and it reinforces a system of masculinity that denies males their feelings and experiences; at the same time, it tells females that they are the only ones who can be victimized.

The spate of cases involving the sexual abuse of young and adolescent males by Catholic and Protestant clergymen, which emerged by the late 1980s, has helped to shed light on the long-term effects and seriousness of such abuse. Numerous courageous adult men and women have gone public, speaking eloquently to the church hierarchies and to the media, about the psychological effects of this exploitation on their lives. Their disclosures have forced religious institutions to accept responsibility for the behavior of some of their leaders, and to adopt protocol for preventing and responding to such abuses. At the same time, these male survivors have established a model for other male victims to follow.

Counselors who treat male sex abuse victims have also begun to write more about the problems their clients have encountered. The reading list at the end of this book will be useful to you in learning more about male victimization.

Mothers find it helpful to have their sons talk to a counselor who is trained to work with male victims and who is comfortable with varied sexual orientations, so that all fears and feelings can be expressed and dealt with in a safe context. It contributes to the male child's healing when the mother is able to treat her son's abuse seriously and to put the appropriate pressure on the legal and helping systems to treat this case just as they would one involving a female victim.

IF YOU ARE A LESBIAN MOTHER

Lesbian mothers say that their sexual orientation sometimes becomes an issue in dealing with their child's sexual abuse. This commonly occurs in incest cases, when the offender has been the father. He may try to use the mother's sexuality as a way of getting custody of the child (i.e., saying that she is an unfit mother) and claim that she is only accusing him of sexual abuse because she wants the child. The mother's sexuality may also be noticed if she takes her partner with her to report the abuse, or to counseling. Having a secure support network intact will be essential under these circumstances, as will an attorney who is familiar with lesbian custody issues in incest cases.

SELF-CARE THROUGH PLANNING

You have the right to get through your child's molestation with your integrity, selfhood, and feelings intact. This will not happen by itself. Mother survivors suggest that once you are through the crisis stage of the molestation that you should make a "personal plan" and follow it religiously. The main ideas are to save time each day for your own thoughts, to establish a support network, and to get out from under the responsibilities associated with mothering once in a while. Here's a generic plan to help you.

Step 1   Schedule time to yourself each day. Write it on the calendar.

Step 2   Define what will happen during this time each day (you can use the time for something different each day, but you must write down what that is).

Step 3   Make sure that your personal time is something that your children know about and respect. Take time away from your children ocasionally. Ask a friend or relative to keep the kids, if you need to.

Step 4   Don't let money be an excuse not to take this time—do something that is inexpensive (like taking a walk or reading, or visiting a friend) if you need to.

Step 5   Enjoy yourself!

By the way, when your children see that you are coping and recovering, they may gain a sense of confidence in knowing things are stabilizing. Taking time for you will contribute to your child(ren)'s health, too.

KEEP A RECORD

Many mothers keep a diary of their child's molestation and their reactions to it. The diary can include court papers, police statements, press clippings, and other documents, as well as your own jottings. You don't have to be a writer to become your own historian. Keeping a record will help you to grasp the reality of what is happening and it will, in time, help you see how far you have come in surviving it all. By all means, keep the names of the people you are meeting, the feelings you are having, and what you are learning.

4.

Legal Issues

There have been many legal developments related to child sexual victimization in the last few years. This chapter tries to summarize the major ones and to give other basic information to help you deal with this aspect of your child's molestation. The information here is primarily concerned with *criminal law* (which involves the breaking of laws and the investigation and trial that follows). But there will also be short discussions of *civil legal procedures* in relation to child sexual abuse. Civil law is concerned with the civil (or private) rights of individuals, as well as with wrongs committed against one person by another that may or may not involve the breaking of laws. (See the discussion below.)

Who establishes laws. Most laws related to child sexual abuse are passed by state legislatures (called general assemblies in some states); thus, these laws vary greatly from state to state. Congress has also passed some relevant laws at the federal level, and, in some cities and counties, publicly elected councils may have enacted ordinances that define certain types of sexual offenses. For this reason, you should consider the information in this chapter general and not necessarily specific to the town where you live. You are strongly encouraged to contact a rape crisis center or women's shelter near you to get legal information specific to your area.

Some things to remember. Sex offenses of all types are against the law. When a law is broken, a crime has been committed. But guilt on the part of the offender must be *proven* in a court of law before he can legally be considered a criminal and be punished or treated through counseling. Only police, prosecutors, and courts have the legal authority to investigate and try offenders, or to determine appropriate punishment. As a citizen, you are reliant on them to do these things—which means you have the right to expect them to perform their duties with sincerity, respect, and effectiveness.

Civil cases. As a citizen, you are entitled to file civil suits against other persons for wrongs that they commit against you—or, in this case, your child. Civil law relies on other cases that form a body of "case law." Civil cases may be heard by a jury or by a judge; the plaintiff (person bringing the case) decides. Winning a civil trial would result in cash or other material settlement from the offender, rather than a sentence of jail or order for treatment. Many sexual assault survivors are seeking civil suits as a means of gaining financial restitution and, quite frankly, revenge on their abusers. To pursue a civil suit, you should secure the services of a lawyer trained specifically in cases involving sexual assault. Some victims pursue a civil case after the criminal case has concluded as a way of collecting damages. However, you may pursue a civil case whether or not a criminal case has occurred, as long as you are within the statute of limitations (that is, you file the suit within the time allowed by your state statutes).

REPORTING THE ABUSE

Who reports it. When and how the molestation is reported is somewhat dependent on who discovers it. If the abuse was discovered by a school official, doctor, or any other professional required by law to report suspected child abuse and neglect, the case may already have been called into authorities by the time you learn about it. It is their responsibility to talk with you about what they have learned, to take your child's statement and your statement, to investigate the allegations, and to follow the legal requirements of the state as far as protecting your child from further abuse. This means that you will be visited by a policeman or state child protective service official. The section "child protective services" in this chapter gives a fuller description about what to expect from this process.

If your child tells a third person—for example, a friend's mother or a neighbor—there is a better chance that you will learn about the abuse in time to make your own report. This will also be true if your child tells you directly. But be aware that anyone can report suspected child abuse, so there are no guarantees that you will be called before authorities are contacted.

Why reporting is important. Reporting is a very significant aspect of addressing what has happened to your child. There are several reasons that you should report the abuse. First, you will want to assure that this doesn't happen to your child (or other children) again. Second, you will want to make sure that the abuser is either punished or treated by a qualified therapist. Third, you will want to make the strongest demonstration possible to your child that what has happened is wrong and that you are standing up for her (or him). Reporting is a key to getting anything done about the abuse, since, as an individual, you lack the legal power to see that the offender is investigated, arrested, tried either treated or punished. Only official agencies of the state have the authority to make these things happen.

Mothers sometimes don't want to report. Some mothers want to avoid reporting, for various reasons. If the offender was a stranger, the mother may have little solid information to report. Also, if the offender is not a member of the family, the mother may believe that she can protect her child against further abuse.

If the offender is someone in the family, mothers often fear disrupting the family's stability. This is especially true if the offender is the breadwinner. Some women may lack confidence in dealing with "authori-ty" figures and powerful people, which they perceive police and other agency personnel to be. Others fear that their children will be taken from them and placed in foster care. Some mothers worry that they will be accused of having a role in the abuse (of being the so-called "silent partner"). Women who did suspect the abuse was happening and didn't do something about it earlier already feel guilt and shame about the situation, and they want to avoid further humiliation by questions from authorities. Many times women are just generally mistrustful of authorities —especially men in high positions. Women who are from racial or ethnic minority backgrounds may worry that they will be treated with less respect and fairness by "the system" than white families. This worry of unequal justice also arises if the abuser is non-white. In other words, a woman may recognize that the legal system is harsher toward ethnic minority criminals and worry that by reporting the crime, she will be inflicting unusually tough punishment on her child's offender.

Making agencies responsible. All of these are logical, even legitimate, concerns. But the seriousness of what has happened, and your lack of legitimate authority to address it, make reporting a matter to contend with. Public agencies should be responsible, fair, respectful, and appropriate in protecting and serving you and your family. You are entitled to this and have the right to expect and demand it. Social movements to stop rape and child sexual abuse these last two decades have focused heavily on appropriate responses from legal systems. Therefore, personnel in law enforcement and social service agencies have received better training in working with victims, families, and offenders than in the old days. You can't be sure even now, of course, that you won't encounter a racist, inept, or corrupt system, but you can be better assured that there are some groups around to help you stand up for proper treatment.

ONE MOTHER'S LEGAL SUCCESS STORY

Women report all sorts of inequalities and horrors in dealing with the legal and helping service systems. But they are standing up to them. One woman's story is worth noting:

> *Carmen was up against a criminal justice system in which many of the agency personnel and lawyers in her rural community were either related to or were good friends with her husband, whom she had accused of molesting the eldest of her two young daughters. To make matters worse, her husband's family also decided to gang up on her and claim she was lying. The story that her husband and his family told was that she made up the story of the abuse so she could get sole custody of the girls in the divorce, which had been pending for a couple of years. Even though she reported the abuse, and charges were filed against her husband, the case continued to stall in the courts as judges disqualified themselves one after another for being her husband's relative or friend. She was truly the outsider. So she left and went back to a state where her family and friends lived. She took the girls with her.*

> *Legal problems followed her, since her husband still had legal visitation rights. But she insisted in keeping her cross-country distance to avoid this. Carmen even served a short jail sentence rather than take the children back to see their father. While she was in jail, a judge in her new community took an interest in her case. He was able to gain custody rights for her. Though deeply in debt and emotionally exhausted, Carmen and her two daughters were able to start over. Carmen found a good job, a supportive environment, and hope. By changing their family name, she was also able to escape further media attention and could have privacy once again.*

DEFINITIONS OF CRIMES

Your child's assault will be categorized under a statute (law) that is supposed to best fit what the evidence shows has happened to her or him. States in which sexual assault laws have been overhauled usually divide crimes—rape and other forms of sexual offenses—against minors from those against adults. Minors are persons under the age of sexual consent, which is 16 in most states. States may also define sexual offenses as lesser crimes (called *misdemeanors*) and more serious crimes (called *felonies*). The particular statute under which a suspected offender is charged will determine which jurisdiction will handle the case.

The specific charges against your child's offender may "change" in the course of events. Police will investigate allegations that they give a name like child molestation or sexual abuse of a minor. But once they have gathered the evidence and taken statements from all the parties, police forward their reports to the prosecutor or district attorney. The prosecutor's office determines the actual charges for which the suspected offender will be tried. Prosecutors usually decide this on the basis of what they believe they can win in court. If the evidence is strong for a serious offense, this may be the crime for which they try to convict the offender. If the evidence looks marginal, or they believe the witnesses seem unlikely to give strong appearances in court, they may seek lesser charges. Prosecutors are supposed to represent the interests of those who have been abused. Through intense public pressure, prosecutors have become increasingly likely to rigorously pursue child sexual abuse offenders.

DEALING WITH
LEGAL PROCEEDINGS

The ways and extent to which you will be involved in the legal events depends in part on who has molested your child. If the offender is not a family member, you may be treated as a more objective party than if your child's offender is a family member. If the offender is outside the family, you may be more likely to be allowed to attend court proceedings and get information from police and prosecutor.

However, you are entitled to ask questions about legal charges and prosecutor strategies throughout the case. If you believe that the police and prosecutors are not being thorough or fair, you may ask them to explain their reasoning and decisions to you. You may also ask them to explain definitions, terminology, and anything else that you don't understand. You are also entitled to put pressure on legal authorities whom you may believe are being unresponsive, but you may want to do this tactfully and as a last resort so as to retain a good working relationship with them as long as possible. Any "problems" that you experience may be more easily resolved if you have a legal advocate from a rape crisis center assist you through this process. Legal advocates are familiar with the legal procedures and can explain what is happening. They can help you get what you and your child need. Most important, they can also provide emotional support at a very stressful time.

CHILD PROTECTIVE SERVICES

Responsibility and training of personnel. State agencies called Child Protective Services (or something similar, depending on the state) are responsible for assuring that child neglect and abuse allegations are investigated and that the children involved are protected from further harm. CPS caseworkers or representatives generally have a college degree in a field related to social work, psychology, or sociology. They have also probably received training in child sexual abuse, as it has been studied and treated for the past 20 years—in other words, they are probably better prepared to serve you and your child than they would have been a decade ago. While this is not a certainty, you have some reason to believe that they are informed about the problems that you are faced with. Hopefully, they are also caring and sensitive.

CPS is nearly always involved in cases where sexual abuse has occurred within the family. CPS caseworkers are typically on hand when mothers are notified about the abuse, and they are the ones who make the administrative arrangements for the child's protection. CPS does not have legal authority in most states to either investigate a case or to remove a child from a home; that is the responsibility of police and sheriff's officials. However, CPS caseworkers may make the *recommendation* that a child be removed and placed in foster care, or that the suspected offender should leave the home (a preferred option in most instances to child removal). CPS personnel may also be on hand during sentencing time to make recommendations about treatment for offender and family members and to keep records on these events. Although CPS personnel play critical advisory and administrative roles in incest cases, they have limited official investigative and legal roles.

Removal of child. A decade ago, many CPS agencies routinely recommended that a child be removed from a family where incest was suspected, in order to assure the child's protection. Nowadays, the suspected abuser is more likely to be the one to be asked to leave while the case is under investigation. However, child removal and temporary placement in a foster home is sometimes still recommended, especially in cases where the mother is believed to be unsupportive of the child, or where the child expresses a wish to leave the family.

You should know exactly what the law requires in case your child is removed. Ask for written information about the legal process and your rights as a parent in this process. In most states, the CPS caseworker assigned to your child's case may ask for foster care for the child up to 72 hours (three days). Within that time frame, the CPS worker must file: (1) a second written report recommending that the child be returned to the "custodial parent"; or (2) a "dependency petition" seeking a longer period of foster care. The purpose of the 72-hour period is to allow a police investigation to take place.

Again, make sure you understand your state's laws covering hearings, time frames, and parental rights if your child should be taken from the home. Also be aware if your child is entitled to a legal representative called a guardian ad litem (GAL) and if you are entitled to a state-paid lawyer or other representative. A rape crisis legal advocate can explain all of these concerns to you.

CPS demands and stresses. As reports of child sexual abuse (and other kinds of child abuse) have increased through the years due to greater public concern, the demands on CPS agencies have grown dramatically. At the same time, many agencies' budgets have remained the same or been slashed. CPS caseworkers are often stretched with heavy case loads and insufficient time to give their clients. These are conditions that you may notice if you encounter this agency after your child's assault.

FAMILY COURTS

If the child's molestation is disclosed during the course of divorce proceedings between you and your husband, the child's custody may be decided in a family court. The family court may also be involved later on (usually after the molestation trial's conclusion) in deciding the terms of visitation, if there are to be any.

A Typical Sequence of Legal Events

1. **The report is made**—to police either by you or another person. In incest cases, the reporter may be a school official or another third party.

2. **The child's safety is determined.** In the case of incest, a CPS case-worker will be assigned to your child's case and will make an initial assessment of her or his safety. The report that comes from this may recommend either that the suspected offender leave the home or the child be removed for 72 hours to allow a police investigation to occur. (Be aware that if your child is removed and temporarily placed in a foster home, you are entitled to a shelter hearing within a given amount of time to determine future custody. In some states, this occurs within 72 hours, but you may need to request it.)

3. **The police investigation takes place.** In incest cases, this happens quickly, usually within 72 hours. In nonfamilial cases, the investigation may be slower and, in fact, could take weeks. In either type of case, the investigation will require that all parties, including the child, give statements. In many communities, the police try to work in a team with prosecutor and CPS workers so that the child only has to give a statement once and, then, in a safe setting with questioning by some-one trained to conduct such interviews. If the interview is conducted in a room with a one-way glass, the mother is sometimes allowed to witness the interview. If you plan to be present at your child's inter-view, you may want to have a legal advocate from the local rape crisis center with you to explain what is happening and to give you emo-tional support.

4. **Interview and possible arrest of alleged offender.** The accused—or alleged—offender (suspect) is interviewed by police and may be arrested. At this point, this person has the option of signing a voluntary confession, admitting what he has done. He may also deny it. (Note: In communities where prosecutors are more likely to prosecute sexual abuse cases on the basis of children's statements, there are higher rates of voluntary confessions and guilty pleas by offenders.) Voluntary confessions have the advantage of allowing the offender to avoid going to court, which spares him and his family the trauma of publicity and emotional duress. In many states, voluntary confessions are also likely to result in treatment instead of jail time.

5. **Charges filed by prosecutor.** In cases where the offender does not make a voluntary confession, the prosecutor will file documents informing the suspect that charges will be filed against him (and specifying those charges). The prosecutor sets an arraignment date.

in Cases Involving Child Molestation

6. **Suspect is arraigned.** The suspected offender is required to appear at a court hearing in which charges are presented to him and he (usually through his lawyer) enters a plea of guilty or not guilty. You may want to check to see if you are permitted to attend this event.

7. **Pretrial hearings are held.** These occur between the arraignment and the trial in order for the prosecutor and defendant's attorney to file documents and negotiate the details of the official trial. You and your child will probably not be allowed to attend these events. (Note: The suspected offender is called the "defendant" once the hearings and trial begin.)

8. **Dependency fact-finding hearing is held.** In incest cases, where the child has been placed in short-term foster care, there is a second hearing at which a juvenile judge determines the child's continued placement. This is also sometimes called the "45-day" hearing (the number of days may vary from state to state). This hearing takes place in juvenile court and is a civil (not criminal) action.

9. **Criminal trial.** The trial will be held in superior court in the jurisdiction where the offense allegedly occurred. The prosecuting attorney handling the case should talk extensively to you and your child about what to expect and how to answer questions. This advance preparation is extremely important for an effective case. You may ask questions to the prosecuting attorney about anything you need more information about, and you should ask whether you or your child will be called on to testify. If either of you will testify, you should ask to see the courtroom ahead of time and, if you wish, to be allowed to role-play the questions and answers. You may want your legal advocate from the rape crisis center to accompany you to these events to help support you and to give you more information. During the trial, you and your child will only be required to be in the courtroom during the time you testify. (Note: In cases where there has been severe emotional abuse to the victim, judges sometimes allow the victim's testimony to be presented through a videotaped interview. This spares the child from further trauma of having to tell her or his story in public and from having to answer confusing, hurtful questions by the defendant's attorney.)

   The trial will result in a jury decision of guilt or acquittal. In some trials, where new facts are discovered through the testimony of witnesses, the charges may change in the course of the trial proceedings. This usually results in the prosecutor charging a lesser crime. In other trials, the defense attorney approaches the prosecutor (outside the courtroom) and asks to work out a plea bargain. In other words, the defendant has decided to admit some form of responsibility. Some states do not permit plea bargains in criminal trials involving felonies.

YOUR RIGHTS AS A PARENT
IN THE LEGAL PROCESS

Keep in mind that you have certain specific and implied rights in legal procedures associated with your child's molestation.

Information. You have the right to ask CPS, police, prosecutor, and any other official person to explain the status of your child's case, when events will occur, and anything else you wish to know.

Advocacy. You are entitled to take a person of your choice to any and every meeting or other event related to your child's case where you must be present. You are also entitled to have an advocate of your choice assist you in gathering information you need. This person may be a legal advocate at a rape crisis center or another person you trust.

Confidentiality. You have the right to expect the details of your and your child's life and experiences to be kept confidential by various agency personnel who are involved. Except for details specifically required for the legal proceedings, one agency is not supposed to divulge private information to any other party without your written consent.

In the event that the offender is arrested, the local newspaper (or other media) may write or broadcast stories based on the police report. Stories may include the suspect's name and charges against him. Most news media do not publish the names of victims; however, you may be contacted by reporters asking for interviews. You are entitled to either grant the interview or to deny it. You may also ask reporters not to use your or your child's name, but be aware that reporters are not bound to grant anonymity to sources they quote. Sometimes it is helpful to ask a rape crisis advocate to attend an interview with you, so she can give the reporter general information about child sexual assault and allow you to concentrate more on personal experience. You may also want to check out the reporters who call you to see if their reporting on these issues have been well-informed and sensitive to the victims.

Contact with the child in foster care. You have the right to have contact with your child during the time she or he is in foster care, unless a judge has specifically forbidden such contact. The CPS caseworker assigned to your case generally arranges visits between child and family. Your child may also call home to talk with family members.

CIVIL SUITS AGAINST OFFENDERS

The role of lawyers. Victims and their families began to use civil suits as one way of seeking restitution from and retribution against child sex offenders in the late 1970s. To file a civil suit, you need an attorney who understands case law related to sex offenses and has demonstrated her or his interest in victims of these type of crimes. Attorneys vary in their financial arrangements on such cases. Some are able to take the cases *pro bono*; in other words, their firms are large enough to be able to represent some clients who have no money to pay legal fees. Others may be able to take your case *on contingency*—to wait until the trial is over and then take a percentage of any money awarded to you. But many will want to charge *regular fees*, which pertain to any consultations with you (in person or by phone), research, travel to court, time in court, etc.

Seeking damages. As the mother of a victim, you would be pursuing the civil case on behalf of yourself and your child. What you can ask for in "damages" from the offender in a civil suit will relate to your wish to be reimbursed for counseling, other expenses, or emotional harm that you and your child have suffered. Your attorney will help you identify the dollar amount you seek.

Over the last decade, more and more adult women have pursued civil suits against men who sexually abused them in childhood. The success rate of adult victims winning such cases has been very good.

Backlash to civil suits. Civil suits involving adult victims have come to public attention not only because there are many successful ones but because accused offenders and their lawyers have decided to rebel. The most controversial of the contested cases are those in which women sued their offenders after remembering their childhood abuse years later. Accused men and their lawyers have tried to publicly discredit what they call "false memory syndrome." They accuse therapists of being profit-motivated and of putting the ideas about sexual abuse into the heads of their clients. The accused offenders usually deny that they sexually abused the person pursuing these cases. Some of the women who have brought civil suits remembered what happened to them during the course of counseling for personal problems, the causes of which were unclear when they first came to their therapist.

A controversy which has attracted considerable media attention—not all of it resulting in informed reporting, unfortunately—is whether victims in fact repress memories of traumatic events in early life as a way of coping. Defense lawyers have had limited success arguing that women lie and that therapists put them up to it as a way of getting money from innocent men. But the controversy is expected to continue on for some time, because it fits within a larger conservative backlash against legal (and other) gains made by women over the last three decades. Incidentally, denunciations of false memory syndrome have also arisen in other nations, most notably the United Kingdom.

RECENT FEDERAL AND STATE LEGAL DEVELOPMENTS

A number of dramatic cases have pushed many state legislatures and the federal Congress to pass laws that strengthen the protection of children against sexual predators.

Stalking laws try to stop one person from following, harassing, and threatening the safety of another person. The specific terms of the law will vary among states that have passed such laws. A victim (or in this case you, the mother, on the victim's behalf) can report stalking to police, who may help you seek a court order preventing the accused person from committing this behavior. If the behavior continues, you should report it to police so they can arrest the individual. Keep in mind that a court order is a piece of paper and may or may not prevent a deranged, compulsive person from stalking (and harming) your child.

Community notification laws are also called "Megan's laws," after 7-year-old Megan Kanka of New Jersey who was stalked, raped, and murdered in 1994, by a convicted sex offender who had served time for child molesting. Forty-five states—33 of them since Megan's death—have passed laws of one kind or another requiring convicted child sex offenders to register with police and allowing—some even mandating—police, in turn, to notify the residents of those communities. A new federal law strengthens state laws by making it easier for citizens to get information about convicted sexual predators.

The effectiveness of community notification laws has been questioned by some. Is it really possible to protect children from our neighbors, co-workers, etc.? The laws have also been successfully challenged in a number of state courts by men who believe they have served their debts to society and deserve their privacy. They also charge that subjecting them to public scrutiny subjects them to a second punishment, something outlawed by the Constitution. But child advocacy groups say the laws have been helpful in protecting many children and that concerned citizens should fight for their survival. One value of having the laws, advocacy groups say, is that they help to overcome the old myth that children are molested by "dangerous strangers." On the contrary, children are molested by persons they know and may live near. Basic information about potentially harmful persons, they argue, better enables parents to act responsibly.

References

Bennett, Mary Jo. (1995, March/April). "Out of the Box: A Family Therapist's Approach to the 'False Memory Syndrome'," *Treating Abuse Today*, Vol. 5, No. 2, pp. 8-17.

Hampson, Rick. "Notification: Reason for law is its biggest problem," *USA Today*, May 14, 1997, pp. A1-A2.

Mayer, Adele. (1993). *Incest: A Treatment Manual for Therapy with Victims, Spouses, and Offenders* (second edition). Holmes Beach, FL: Learning Publications, Inc.

Orr, Marjorie (Hons). (1995, May/June). "Accuracy about Abuse: The 'False Memory Syndrome' Debate in the United Kingdom, *Treating Abuse Today*, Vol. 5, No. 3, pp. 19-27+.

"Sexual Assault Within the Family," (pamphlet; no date). Seattle, WA: Sexual Assault Center, Harborview Hospital.

Strong, Marilee. (1997). "Monsters in Our Midst," World Wide Web (*http://www.diablopubs.com/focus/ARCHIVES/FEATURES/sexoffenders.html*).

Incest patterns have changed less than any other form of family violence over the last century. This does not mean that incest is a pathology uninfluenced by historical change, but that the social arrangements that give rise to it have been tenacious.

Linda Gordon
professor of American History
University of Wisconsin–Madison*

* Linda Gordon, *Heroes of Their Own Lives: The Politics and History of Family Violence.* New York, NY: Penguin Books, p. 210.

5.

Culture and Class

A mother's cultural background and socioeconomic class can affect her experience with her child's sexual molestation, as well as her own survival and healing. This chapter presents basic information and also explores some of the experiences that mothers have shared in relation to their cultural and socioeconomic identities. Thinking more intentionally about your own background and social status in relation to your child's abuse may help you to understand what you are going through and to develop coping strategies for surviving that are appropriate and reasonable for you. You may also find useful information in Chapter 6, Religious Issues, if your cultural background involves Christian or Judaic belief systems.

WHAT ARE CULTURE AND CLASS?

Culture. Everyone has a cultural background and identity, even though we may not have thought much about it or we have grown away from our origins. Culture, as used in this chapter, refers to the traditions, beliefs, values and ways of life that are learned from our parents, families, and communities. Our culture may be determined by a combination of ethnic, racial, national, regional, religious, and other influences. Most of us expand our cultural identities as we mature through what we learn to appreciate and enjoy in terms of lifestyles, tastes, and so forth, beyond those we grew up with.

Your cultural background has helped to shape the way you understand and think about your child's abuse, just as it has other events in your life. You may find your cultural traditions helpful or a hindrance to you. Perhaps you will think they are simply irrelevant.

Class. Similarly, everyone belongs to a socioeconomic class. We don't talk about class much in the United States, because there is a common belief that we are a "classless society" in which "everyone is born equal" or at least that everyone has the same opportunity to get ahead. In fact, the U.S. is a nation deeply defined—some would even say divided— by socioeconomic class. By class we mean social standing that is generally determined by income, educational level, our parents' social status, and certain other factors (for example, whether we have close associations with persons of prestige and power).

It's possible to move out of the socioeconomic class into which we are born, whether that be through upward or downward mobility. For instance, someone born into a lower-income family may be able to advance through education and employment, by investing wisely, or by winning the lottery. It's also possible that someone born into a middle or higher socioeconomic class could slip downward through loss of income or other misfortune. Persons born into poverty, however, stand the least chance of changing socioeconomic status. Since the 1980s, class divisions have become more pronounced in the U.S., with the gap between rich and poor growing wider. The numbers of persons living at or below the poverty line continue to increase, and personal debts are rising steadily (particularly through credit card use). Women are the most likely to be low-income or poor, because they still earn less than men even after several decades of legal and other social reforms to advance women's equality.

Women, culture, and class will be discussed at greater length below, particularly in relation to child molestation.

CULTURAL HERITAGE
AS A SUPPORT

Many women find their cultural heritage a source of great strength in this time of crisis. Some ethnic communities have traditional support systems in place that women are already a part of and can readily employ, both practically and spiritually.

Marlene, who lived on an Indian reservation and participated regularly in a women's circle, looked to her tribal sisters for advice and empathy when her 7-year-old daughter was molested by her uncle. The members of the circle also assisted her in getting tribal leaders to take legal action against the offender.

Anastasia's Ukrainian family had always closely observed its nation's cultural religious (Eastern Orthodox) customs. Anastasia, too, carried on these traditions after marrying and having her own children. When her 4-

year-old daughter was molested by a neighbor in the springtime, Anastasia said she "kept myself sane" by teaching her older children the elaborate methods used by Ukrainians to paint Easter eggs. Everyone had a project, and the work "lifted our spirits," she said, while the legal process was going on.

A number of ethnic communities have also *broken* cultural traditions in order to better protect children and support their mothers (and other family members). In the Seattle area, for example, members of the various Asian communities* recognized that quite a few children of Asian descent were being molested by non-Asian persons. They theorized that traditional teachings, such as obeying elders and maintaining silence about shameful things (such as sexual violation), made their children more vulnerable to assault and prevented them from telling someone (and getting help) if they were molested. By working with local rape crisis programs, members of several Asian community services developed educational programs about child sexual assault for both parents and children in several languages. They also created culture-specific crisis services, which included translators and advocates to assist mothers (and other family members) with police and other agencies.

CULTURAL DILEMMAS

Invisibility and silence around problems of abuse. Mothers have not always found solace in their cultures. Some mothers belong to communities where abuse of women and children has been less visible, and may even have been denied. The silence that surrounds child molestation sends a message that these are not things to be talked about if they happen. Silence is one factor that has contributed to low reporting in African-American, Hispanic, and other ethnic minority communities. In the last few years, however, women from within these communities have begun to talk about and write about the problems.

Mistrust of agencies. Underreporting of child sexual abuse to police, or even not seeking emergency services through rape crisis centers, may be due to a mistrust of these agencies. Mistrust arises when we look at agency personnel who are, by and large, different from us and who

---

*Seattle's large, diverse Asian community is composed of persons who were either born in or descended from natives of the Philippines, Japan, China, Korea, Thailand, Vietnam, Cambodia, Laos, India, Tibet, Malaysia, the Paciific Islands, and elsewhere.

have a history of not treating our group's members fairly. An African-American mother might ask herself, "How can my family expect to get justice or support from people who don't understand us?" or "...who will not give us the same attention as [that white family]?" Today, persons in many rape crisis centers, CPS, police, and other agencies have had training in cultural awareness. Many have also strived to hire a culturally diverse staff. This hasn't always been true. Yolanda's story is typical of how things used to be too often, and may remain so today in some instances:

> *When Yolanda went to Child Protective Services a number of years ago with her two daughters to give their statements about how their father had molested them, she was accompanied by her neighbor Charlotte. Charlotte had offered to go as Yolanda's friend and supporter. However, throughout the interview the CPS worker directed many of her questions to Charlotte rather than to Yolanda or the girls—as if her questions needed translation. Charlotte, in turn, would turn and restate the questions to whomever was meant to answer them. Yolanda and her girls were of Mexican-American descent; the CPS worker and Charlotte were both white. English was Yolanda's and the girls' first language, but they spoke English with a slight accent.*
>
> *The situation was incredibly awkward, tense, and demeaning, Yolanda said later. She wanted the girls to give their statement, because she believed them and wanted to keep them from further abuse. But she also wanted the CPS worker to treat her and the girls like equals. Yolanda said that she began to cry at one point during the session out of frustration. She had many questions to ask the CPS person but was too embarrassed; she worried that she would seem stupid. At the end of the interview, she was told that the girls would have to give their statement again, next time to a policeman. Yolanda left not knowing why or when, or what would happen with her husband, Pedro. She and the girls went home that night to Pedro and worried he would find out they had reported the abuse before the police came to arrest him. Yolanda called a rape crisis center the following day and was able to talk with a child advocate about the abuse and what was happening in the reporting process.*

Yolanda had encountered a professional who was uncomfortable with her and her girls' cultural identities. Fortunately, Yolanda was assertive enough to see through the problem and seek support for herself. The next time she saw the CPS worker, she had a list of questions to ask that the advocate had helped her prepare.

Some mothers aren't able to be as forthright as Yolanda. They may have been subjected to too many experiences in the past that gave them little faith in "the system." Their answer is to avoid any contact whatsoever with police and other professionals and to devise their own plan to protect their children.

Racial discrimination is real, not imagined. Many mothers realize that the kind of indignities that Yolanda was subjected to is part of a deeply entrenched system of racial and ethnic prejudice and discrimination. It's a fact that the nation's prisons are full of men who are mainly of Black, Hispanic, and mixed racial origins. Women from these communities rightfully worry that they and their families may not get the same benefits, privileges, and protection as those in the white majority culture. Similarly, mothers may have concern that the child's offender, if he is an ethnic minority, may be treated more harshly for his crime than a white offender might be. If that offender is a family member or a teenager, this could lessen a mother's desire to let authorities know.

Stigmatizing the community. Mothers of molested children (like adult victims of sexual assault and domestic violence) may also worry that, by making others aware of the abuse, she will be bringing negative attention to a minority community. This, she may fear, will just further stigmatize or bring dishonor to her community or group.

Avoiding shame. Some women have not sought services or reported their children's abuse because they have internalized the mistaken belief that sexual abuse is something the victim brings on herself or himself. They may feel deep shame for what has happened and believe they should keep their shame to themselves rather than dishonor an entire family or community.

SURVIVAL ISSUES RELATED TO CULTURE AND CLASS

It is difficult to generalize about the ways in which culture and class will affect your own experience after your child is molested. You have your own personal values, traditions, stories, and healing systems that will affect how you think about and understand what has happened. If you encounter difficulties, you may find it useful to think of the many others who have also been through this situation.

The women—and many supportive men—who have worked tirelessly through the years to address child victimization, such as your child has experienced, have been diverse in their cultural and socioeconomic backgrounds. They include past victims (survivors) and mothers of victimized children, like yourself. This is to say that women of all ethnicities and income levels have cared about stopping child molestation and of making the criminal justice system, child protective service agencies, counselors, and others responsive and accountable to you and others they serve. As discussed in Chapter 4, Legal Issues, you are extremely limited in your authority when dealing with someone who molests children. Therefore, you have to look to the professionals invested with the public trust to take action to protect your child and to deal with the offender. You have the right to expect them to do a good job for you.

You also have the right to be appreciated for who you are by those you talk to in your personal circles—family, friends, acquaintances, co-workers—if you decide to tell them.

THE SOCIOECONOMICS
OF MOTHERS' EXPERIENCES

Resources can make a difference. Class standing can affect women's options when they learn their children are molested. Mothers who have access to sufficient economic resources (health insurance or money) can seek professional counseling for their child (and perhaps themselves) because they have the means of paying for it. If the child's offender is the husband or partner, a mother with resources can more easily decide to leave him than perhaps a woman who is solely reliant on her child's abuser for income. Mothers who come from supportive families with adequate or ample finances may be willing to help them through a rough time while they get a job and start a new life. Mothers who are already gainfully employed, who earn enough income to support themselves and their children, may also have an easier time than women without funds. Baby-sitters, movies, trips out of town to "get away from it all," and meals away from home are all easier to come by with enough money.

When resources are lacking. What about mothers who don't have access to financial resources?

Many women have spent years at home raising children and being reliant upon a husband or partner's income. If this is you, you may have had little access to bank accounts or other resources you can call your own. If you weren't married to your partner who molested your child(ren), perhaps you had no health insurance to take yourself or your children to the doctor. Many women like yourself understandably worry that you will subject yourself and your families to poverty if you leave a sexually abusive mate.

Getting what's yours. While this is a legitimate worry, it is also one that can keep you and your child(ren) stuck in a harmful situation. Battered women's shelters, displaced homemakers groups, legal service agencies for low-income persons, and even many community colleges have staff who are well-versed in circumstances like your own. They can help you think through economic strategies for survival and even point you to possible sources of income to help you get what is rightfully yours. These "rights" may include getting your fair share of the offender's income or assets, as well as perhaps a job training program for yourself (if you haven't been in the paid work force for a while).

You should also know that many states have victims' compensation programs through which you can apply for funds to pay for counseling and other expenses associated with the sexual abuse.

If you do have health insurance, you and your children may want to explore counseling to help you cope with what has happened. Most insurance programs pay for designated numbers of visits with qualified therapists.

If you are employed by a company or agency of some size, you may want to see if your place of work has special "employee assistance programs" to assist you in some way. These are usually confidential.

SOME ADDITIONAL THOUGHTS

Our cultural and socioeconomic backgrounds contribute much to who we are, how we see the world, how we operate in that world, and the kind of power we perceive that we have. Culture and class may also affect our access to services, justice under the law, and, perhaps our perceptions of what we are entitled to. An essential part of surviving your child's sexual molestation will be:

▸ *feeling as if you have the right to tell someone* what has happened, whether within your community, family, friendship circle, or outside these;

▶ *being listened to and supported* in your needs and your right to make choices (within the legal limits in some cases);

▶ *getting fair and respectful treatment* from all the agencies you come into contact with; this includes information that you need to help you make choices and to understand what is being done, as well as to have your child protected from further harm;

▶ *getting access to the resources you need* to make appropriate choices for yourself and your family; and

▶ *feeling appreciated for yourself*, including your background, beliefs, values, and lifestyle.

6.

Religious Issues

by Rev. Marie M. Fortune *

As a Protestant minister, I have worked since 1976 to teach religious leaders how to respond with sensitivity and compassion to those who have been harmed by sexual or domestic violence. The Center for the Prevention of Sexual and Domestic Violence in Seattle is where we do this work. It is our job to change the ways that pastors and rabbis respond to victims and abusers. During this time, we have seen significant changes in the way that our churches and synagogues address the realities of victimization in our midst. But more change is needed.

There are still pastors or rabbis who say, "But no one ever comes to me with this problem." I'm sure this is true. But why don't they ask themselves, "Why aren't my people coming to me with these problems that I read about in the paper every day?" They have not opened the door and given their people permission to come forward and share their experiences of abuse.

A person's church or synagogue can be a tremendous help to her in time of crisis—or it can be a huge burden. If a religious leader has been trained and understands sexual and domestic violence, then that person will be a great resource. Fortunately, there are more of these pastors and rabbis available than ever before.

* **Rev. Marie M. Fortune** is a minister in the United Church of Christ and Executive Director of the Center for the Prevention of Sexual and Domestic Violence, Seattle, Washington. She is the author of *Sexual Violence: The Unmentionable Sin* (Pilgrim Press, 1983), *Is Nothing Sacred: When Sex Invades the Pastoral Relationship* (Harper & Row, 1989), and *Keeping the Faith: Questions and Answers for the Abused Woman* (Harper & Row, 1987). Although her perspective represents that of a Protestant minister, she seeks to raise issues that stretch across various religious traditions.

As a mother whose child has been molested—probably by someone you know and believed you could trust—you have been through one of the worst nightmares any woman can face. The offender may have been your husband or boyfriend, another relative, a neighbor, teacher, coach or minister. If you are a religious person, you may be struggling with questions about where God is in all of this, or about something you learned in Sunday School many years ago. Here are some common questions that women in your situation ask. Hopefully the responses will be helpful to you.

As you read through these common religious issues that arise in connection with child molestation, you may want to think of these words from Hebrew scripture that give voice to Rachel's grief over the taking of her children into exile and to God's promise that they will return:

> Thus says the Lord:
> A voice is heard in Ramah,
> lamentation and bitter weeping.
> Rachel is weeping for her children,
> because they are no more.

> Thus says the Lord:
> Keep your voice from weeping, and your eyes from tears;
> for there is a reward for your work, says the Lord;
> they shall come back from the land of the enemy;
> there is hope for your future, says the Lord;
> your children shall come back to their own country.

> Jeremiah 31:15-17 (NRSV)

PUNISHMENT AND SUFFERING

Can this be God's will for my child and for me? How can a loving God let this happen to a child? Am I being punished for something I did long ago?

Whenever we experience suffering and pain, it is a natural reaction to ask "Why?" The question of why there is suffering at all is a question that has challenged religious leaders for centuries. Each religious tradition answers it in a different way. The pain that the offender has caused for you and your child is not God's will. The responsibility lies only with the one who caused the harm. Unfortunately, God cannot prevent the sinful acts of a person; God can only call that person to repentance.

You are not being punished and neither is your child. Your child encountered a teen or adult who was not trustworthy at a time when your child was particularly vulnerable. This was not God's doing.

Every time a child suffers or a mother's heart is broken by the pain she sees in her child, God weeps with you. In both Hebrew and Christian scriptures, we learn about a God who stands by the abused, the exploited person—anyone who has been taken advantage of by someone who is bigger and stronger. Without a doubt, God takes your side and your child's side. God shares your tears and your anger, your despair and your hopes for healing.

FORGIVENESS

Many women like yourself ask, "Must I forgive the person who has abused my child?"

No, you are not obligated to forgive and do not ask your child to forgive—unless other things happen first.

For Christians, Jesus' teaching is clear: If someone sins against you, rebuke him, and IF he repents, forgive him (Luke 17:1-4). Repentance here means more than remorse—"I'm sorry, I didn't mean to hurt you," is not enough. Repentance is about change: getting a new heart and a new mind, as the prophet Ezekiel says. Repentance requires hard work and time.

For Jews, the teaching is similar. The rabbis taught that when someone does harm to another person, he or she should not be forgiven unless he or she makes things right by atoning for the wrongdoing, compensating the neighbor for harm done and by bringing an apology and seeking forgiveness. In other words, the one who has caused the harm must take responsibility for what he did and take the initiative in making it right. It is not the victim's responsibility to initiate.

But also remember what forgiveness is: It is letting go of the vivid memories that you and your children can get on with your lives. This does not mean forgetting. I doubt that you or your child will ever forget what happened. If you have experienced some sense of justice, you may be able to put this experience in perspective and move forward. Forgiveness does not mean that the harm that the person did to you or your child will ever be okay.

Let's say that the person who harmed your child has confessed, been in prison or treatment, seems genuinely remorseful, is paying for your child's and your therapy expenses, etc. Let's say that you and your child feel okay about moving on and letting go—in other words, forgiving. This does not mean that you ever have to relate to the offender again or that you should ever trust that person again. That person betrayed you and your child. Forgiving him or her does not mean that you must relate to him/her as if nothing had ever happened.

Quick forgiveness is not good for the offender either. I was invited to meet with a group of 27 incest offenders who were in a court-mandated treatment program. This was a community program, but 25 of the 27 men were active Christians and they wanted to discuss religious questions with a minister. So, we spent an evening in discussion about a variety of topics. At the end of the evening, as the men were summarizing, they said, "Whenever you talk with other clergy, tell them for us not to forgive too quickly."

Each of the 25 Christian offenders, when he was arrested for molesting his child, went immediately to his pastor and asked to be forgiven. All of the ministers prayed over the men and sent them home "forgiven." The offenders said, "It was the worst thing that anyone could ever have done for us. It meant that we didn't have to confront what we had done to our children."

These offenders' witness is very important. They are telling us that premature forgiveness doesn't help them; it doesn't help anyone. In fact, it can prevent them from ever truly repenting and being accountable for what they did.

SEPARATION AND DIVORCE

The person who molested my child was my husband (my child's father). I don't think I can ever live with him again. But I thought the Bible said that divorce is wrong. What should I do?

Different Christian churches have different teachings about divorce. Some allow it and others don't. But what is clear in the Gospels is that Jesus was concerned for the well-being of the woman in marriage. He taught against divorce because he saw husbands casting off wives for no reason except that they were tired of them and wanted a younger woman. He said that husbands could not do this.

Most churches today understand that when someone abuses a family member, he has broken the marriage covenant by that abuse. He has betrayed the trust of members of his family and has broken up his marriage. The woman who is abused by her husband or who is trying to protect her children from their father's abuse is not only allowed but in fact should leave that relationship. You are not breaking up your family, he has already done that. You are just taking action to prevent further harm to yourself and your children.

Even some Roman Catholic bishops are clear on this subject. In 1996, the Roman Catholic bishops of Northern Canada issued a statement reinforcing a married woman's right, and even the duty, to leave a violent relationship to protect herself and her children. The statement acknowledged that while the church believes strongly in the sacredness of marriage, it does not mean to convey women should stay in relationships that are abusive.

The real question as you consider divorce is the meaning of faithlessness. In the book of Malachi in Hebrew Scripture, the prophet says:

And this you do as well: You cover the Lord's altar with tears, with weeping and groaning because [God] no longer regards the offering or accepts it with favor at our hand. You ask, "Why does [God] not?" Because the Lord was a witness between you and the wife of your youth, to whom you have been faithless, though she is your companion and your wife by covenant . . . For I hate divorce, says the Lord, the God of Israel, and covering one's garment with violence, says the Lord of hosts. So take heed to yourself and do not be faithless.

Malachi 2:13-16, 16

God is speaking to husbands: "Don't come crying to me. I know you have been faithless to your wife. I hate it when divorce becomes necessary because of your faithlessness and violence. So keep faith with your wife." Everyone would prefer that husbands be faithful to wives and thus avoid divorce; this is best for everyone. But when a husband brings violence and abuse to his marriage, he is being faithless. And divorce is the likely consequence.

Your job is to protect your children and yourself from further harm. If the only way to do this is to end your relationship with your husband, then that is what you should do.

TELLING YOUR RELIGIOUS COMMUNITY

What about my church or synagogue? I don't know if I should tell them about all of this.

If you are considering whether and how to share this situation with your pastor or rabbi and the congregation, it is important to think it through carefully. Unfortunately, not every congregation is aware and understanding when it comes to child abuse.

We received a call from a woman who had discovered that her husband was molesting her children. She had had him arrested and then went immediately to her church for support. Instead of providing the support she sought and needed, church leaders told her she could not teach Sunday School anymore and that her children could not attend Sunday School. These same leaders never said a word to the father who was the offender and also an active church member. This was the opposite of what the church leaders should have done. Out of ignorance and fear, they blamed the victims and further victimized them. The mother was hurt and angry when she called us. I doubt if she has ever gone back to any church after the way she was treated.

On the other hand, there was a woman whose husband had abused both her and her child. She went to her church for help. There she found people who helped her find a safe place to stay and supported her financially for the first year while she finished job training and figured out how to survive as a single mom. When it came time for the custody hearing, the pastor and a deacon went with her and testified for her at the hearing. This church community understood the situation and did everything it could to help this woman protect herself and her child.

You can look for a congregation like this one to give you support. You deserve all the help you can find in your community, but you may have to look to find it.

When you go to see your pastor or rabbi, ask if he or she has any training or experience in dealing with child abuse. If not, ask her or him at least to read this book. If she or he seems supportive and sympathetic to you, then you may have found a valuable resource. If you do not find sympathy and support, then look elsewhere.

A JEWISH WOMAN ASKS

I'm Jewish and it was my father who molested my child. My father —her grandfather—is now dead. It is very painful for me to attend Memorial Service (Yizkor). What can I do?

I'm sure that this unfinished business is very painful. You may find this suggested preface for Yizkor services, which was prepared by Marcia Cohn Spiegel, to be helpful:

As we prepare for the Memorial Service, we must acknowledge that for some of us this is a particularly difficult time. Many of us mourn for loved ones whose memories are a blessing; others of us have troublesome memories, unfinished business with those who died. Those of us who have not reconciled ourselves with family members cannot extol their lives, exalt their memories. But we cannot live forever with bitterness, anger or rage in our lives.

While Judaism does not require that we forgive those who have perpetrated evil against us, in order to move toward shlemut, wholeness and personal integrity in our lives, we can use this time of memory for our own personal healing and growth. Kaddish is not a prayer that praises the dead; it is a prayer that praises God and the power of God in the world. As we recite Kaddish together with all Jews all over the world, we remember that death is an inevitable part of life. We mourn those who died before their time, those who died in suffering and pain, those whose lives enriched the world. And, we remember the living, asking healing for all who suffer so that they can move on.[1]

ANGER

I am just so angry at _____ (the abuser). He stole my child's innocence. But I always learned that nice Christian women weren't supposed to be angry. What do I do with these feelings?

It's fine to be angry. Of course, you are angry. How can you not be angry at the abuser for what he did to your child? Remember the story of

---

[1]Marcia Cohn Spiegel, activist and author from Los Angeles, in a personal communication to Marie M. Fortune, December 1, 1996.

Jesus in the temple (John 2:13-17)? Jesus drove the moneychangers out of the temple because they had turned a sacred place into a marketplace. He was certainly angry at the misuse of the temple; and he is certainly angry at the exploitation of your child. Also in Mark 3:1-6, Jesus reacts with anger to those who tried to trick him regarding his healing of the sick on the Sabbath: "He looked around at them with anger; he was grieved at their hardness of heart . . ." I expect this is Jesus' reaction to those who stand by and do little to stop a child abuser.

You may feel like some of your anger is at God. Go ahead and write a letter to God expressing this anger. God can handle it. And God shares your anger.

Your anger at what the abuser did to your child is righteous anger—it appropriate anger. Righteous anger can give you the energy to protect your child and support your child through the healing process. The writer of Ephesians says: "So then, putting away falsehoods, let all of us speak the truth to our neighbors, for we are members of one another. Be angry but do not sin; do not let the sun go down on your anger. . ." (Ephesians 4:25-26) This is about righteous anger which is an expression of the truth of the harm done to a child. The writer is also saying to channel your anger into something productive so that you will not have to carry it forever.

ABUSE BY A CLERGYPERSON

My child was molested by a minister. How can I ever trust the church again?

This is a very good question. You and your child have been betrayed by someone who should have been trustworthy. This should never have happened, but unfortunately, sometimes it does. The important question is this: How is the church handling this? Are the church leaders supportive of you and your child? Are they listening carefully to your concerns? Are they cooperating with any criminal investigation of the report? Are they willing to provide for the counseling for your child? Are they holding the minister accountable and making sure that this person cannot harm anyone else?

If the church leaders are doing these things, then perhaps your faith in the church as a whole can be renewed. If they are not, then they have lost an opportunity to minister with you and there is no reason that you should trust them in the future.

The problem of child sexual abuse by priests and ministers only began to surface in the mid-1980s. Generally speaking, complaints were brought forward by adult survivors who had been abused as children. The complaints were not handled well in the beginning. Major law suits won by survivors finally got the churches' attention and policies and procedures have begun to change. This statement from Bishop William G. Curlin of the Roman Catholic Diocese of Charlotte, North Carolina, exemplifies how a religious leader should respond to the abuse of children by priests. He went to the parish where Rev. William Kuder served in the 1950s and made this statement:

> *Some may ask, "Why bring this up now, after so many years following Father Kuder's death? What good can be accomplished by such a revelation? Let me assure you that the victims of Father Kuder and their families have never ceased to feel the intense pain he brought them. Their Calvary has lasted a lifetime and continues to this day. . . . For those who were victims of Father Kuder, I assure you that you were innocent of all sin. You were a child who was abused and molested by a man who hid behind his priesthood and took advantage of it to use you for his personal pleasure. . . . We want to publicly apologize and declare our determination that this will never happen again. We, as a Catholic community, can allow no less than zero tolerance of this evil.*[2]

Bishop Curlin emphasized the diocese's policy, which states that any allegation of sexual abuse against a priest will bring about his immediate removal from ministry pending an investigation and that any priest found guilty of sexual abuse will be expelled from the priesthood with no second chance.[3]

CHURCHES' AND SYNAGOGUES' DUTY

This kind of response reminds us that the church is capable of addressing the sexual abuse of children directly and firmly. We must continue to work to make churches and synagogues safe places for all our children.

---

[2]Tim Reid, "Church Issues Apology," *The Asheville Citizen-Times*, March 6, 1995.

[3]Ibid.

The most important thing for you to remember is that God is present to you as you walk this long and sometimes lonely path. God will never desert you although others may. God can hear your anger and despair. Don't be afraid to pour out your heart in prayer to God. And listen for God's promise:

Thus says the Lord:

Keep your voice from weeping, and your eyes from tears;
for there is reward for your work, says the Lord;
they shall come back from the land of the enemy;
there is hope for your future, says the Lord;
your children shall come back to their own country.

Jeremiah 31-16-17 (NRSV)

NOTE TO READERS:

The Center for the Prevention of Sexual and Domestic Violence has produced the following two videos to help religious communities respond to abuse. Both videos include a 24-page study guide and packet of awareness brochures.

"Hear Their Cries: Religious Responses to Child Abuse" is an award-winning video on the role of clergy and lay leaders in ending child abuse (48 minutes, color, 1992). Order No. V-200, purchase price $129, rental price $40. Call for shipping costs.

"Bless Our Children: Preventing Sexual Abuse" tells the story of one congregation's efforts to include sexual abuse prevention in its children's religious education (40 minutes, color, 1993). Order No. V-201, purchase price $99, rental price $40. Call for shipping costs.

Both videos are available together for a discounted price of $185.00. Order No. V-202, purchase price $185, rental price $60.

Contact the Center for the Prevention of Sexual and Domestic Violence, 936 N. 34th Street, Suite 200, Seattle, WA 98103, (206) 634-1903; FAX (206) 634-0115. Also, visit the Center's web site: *http://www.cpsdv.org*

7.

Recovery

by Muriel Templeton, M.S. *

Mothers whose children have been abused need both confidence and energy at a time when they may have little of either. Therefore, mothers are encouraged to share their needs with their children's counselors. Counselors, in turn, can either include mothers' counseling needs within the scope of the child's support plan or provide an appropriate referral to a local therapist or sexual assault center.

There are several pressing reasons for a mother to have immediate emotional support. The mother's personal recovery from the trauma is essential in and of itself, of course. It is important not only for the mother to have immediate emotional support for her own personal recovery from the trauma, but to gain understanding that belief in their child's disclosure is a powerful factor in the child's recovery and adjustment. Additionally, the dual recovery of both mother and child contribute to a long-term positive child-mother relationship.

COUNSELING ISSUES

While each mother brings her own unique problems and questions into counseling, several common concerns emerge.

Children's Blame and Anger

It is commonly found that when mothers are given the opportunity to deal with their own personal concerns in counseling that, quite often,

---

* Muriel Templeton, M.S., is a certified mental health counselor in the state of Washington. She has been working with survivors and families affected by sexual assault and family violence for twenty years.

the first feeling to emerge is their resentment and confusion over the blame and anger directed at them by their abused daughter or son. It seems that children expect mothers to be able to read minds, to know what is going on without being told. The child may have given a mother vague, indirect messages that all is not well, but only with hindsight can a mother usually "read" the hidden truth of what was going on.

Sometimes it is useful to schedule some joint mother-daughter (or son) sessions, to allow the daughter to express her anger, have it redirected appropriately (toward the offender), and to lay the foundation to prepare for a new way of communicating between mother and child. Children's extreme anger can often be disconcerting for mothers, particularly if they have difficulty expressing their own anger. Joint counseling can become a place where mothers and children both learn to articulate angry feelings and to direct them at the offender, who is really responsible for the problems.

Mother-Child Alienation

Very often, alienation develops between a mother and child. This is usually something that has arisen through the offender's manipulation, as a tactic in facilitating the ongoing abuse. Mothers can use counseling as a place to explore the way this alienation came about and to consider ways of overcoming it. This often becomes an opportunity for mothers and daughters, in particular, to develop a new, more open relationship that will last and enrich the rest of their lives.

Adolescent Victim Behavior and Loyalty Toward the Offender

In cases of incest, mothers often report their helplessness and confusion when their adolescent daughter begins to act out in a self-destructive way after the disclosure and legal intervention.

Truancy, running away, staying out at night, sexual involvement with older men and strangers, and drug and alcohol abuse are common behaviors with adolescent incest victims. Mothers, already feeling inadequate, often become desperate about their inability to protect their daughters from further harm.

It is important to help a mother recognize that adolescents, in particular, still usually feel a loyalty toward the abusive family member. Children are often made to feel "special" by the abuser, which develops the child's dependency on the abuser for favors and preferred treatment. Adolescents are also affected by their perceived "participation" in the sexual abuse. This develops false notions that the child herself/himself has caused the sex to happen. Such confusion results in a lack of self-worth and leads to self-destructive behaviors that may seem "exciting" to the child. An understanding of these issues will help the mother to be more supportive toward her daughter or son, rather than rejecting. It can be helpful to work on ways of developing protective limits for the daughter in counseling sessions, possibly in cooperation with school personnel.

Depression—Overt and Covert

It is important for counselors to recognize when mothers they counsel are suffering from depression. The depression may be chronic (having existed for a long time) or may be precipitated by the recent events associated with the child's abuse. In either case, depression may be compounded by feelings of guilt and hindsight. Women may recognize their depression and be able to talk about it, in which case, the counseling to address underlying causes and remedies is approached more quickly. In cases where women suffering from chronic depression are unaware of their condition, counseling will occur more slowly in order to unravel the complicated conditions that have caused the depression and allowed it to linger unrecognized.

Mothers' Own Victimization

Mothers are often confronted with the need to deal with their own prior sexual victimization after their children are sexually abused. Hearing the child's story may cause a mother to remember her own molestation or incest and to re-experience the anguish, guilt, and other feelings associated with it. Some mothers who have never told anyone about the victimization may be reluctant to do so now, when they feel their job is to comfort their children. In addition, they have spent many years internalizing the shame and self-blame while they have kept the secret of their sexual abuse.

However, many women have found dealing with their own abuse to be a basic starting point in counseling. Once they have talked about their own victimization, they are able to be more responsive to their children. Most women make immediate connections between their past victimization and events in their current lives, once they explore these issues. One such link may be their vulnerability to continued manipulation or abuse by their husbands or partners. Finding ways to deal with the current, related problems is made possible through retrospective therapeutic work.

Parenting

Studies indicate that mothers with a childhood history of sexual abuse often report having difficulty being parents. Growing up in the absence of boundaries for appropriate parent-child behavior leaves them guessing and unconfident about how to provide these for their own children. Therefore, supportive counseling at a time of the child's disclosure can give a mother the opportunity to learn parenting skills that contribute both to her own and her child's self-esteem.

SELECTING A COUNSELOR

You should begin your own counseling experience knowing that you are the expert on your situation. Counselors can help you clarify your problems and support you in making choices, and they can guide you toward more knowledge of child molestation. But, in the end, no one will know more than you do about your life, your thoughts, and feelings than you do. You can remain secure in this fact through your counseling.

Most mothers find either short-term or long-term counseling a necessary part of surviving their child's molestation. Some mothers have had previous experience working with counselors; others are entering the counseling experience for the first time. In selecting a counselor, you have the right to work with a counselor who:

- You are comfortable and safe with and feel is trustworthy

- Respects you and listens to your concerns and feelings

- Supports your own goals and choices, and will affirm your assertiveness in making important choices

- Has experience and training to work with family members hurt by incest or molestation

- Accepts the offender's responsibility for what has happened

- Recognizes and supports you as a whole person, including your cultural and religious beliefs, sexual orientation, education and socioeconomic situation

You may want to make a mental or written list of questions to ask the counselor during your first session that will help you decide if this is the best person for you. You are free to inquire about the counselor's training, philosophy toward molestation and incest, attitudes toward women, and any other matter that concerns you. If cost is a potential problem for you, you may want to ask about sliding scale fees for clients. These questions are best cleared up before the therapy begins. However, you are free to raise questions that concern you and to stop seeing a counselor at any point in your therapy if you feel uncomfortable with the person you are seeing.

Your local sexual assault center should have a list of therapists in your area, along with their qualifications, to aid you in finding a counselor and referring you to a supportive group. Some states include counseling for mothers as part of their crime victims' compensation programs.

STORIES OF MOTHERS' RECOVERIES

Following are four success stories about mother survivors. The names are changed and extensive personal details eliminated in order to protect real identities of women who have not made their situations generally known in their communities.

Story #1: MARG

Marg, whose two children, a boy and a girl, were sexually abused by their father, went through extended individual and family counseling for more than two years. While Marg and her husband divorced the year after the disclosure, they wanted to work together in family therapy for the children's sake. I asked Marg, "When do you think all this will be over?" She said immediately, "Never." But she said it with a sort of lightness and talked with a laugh indicating all the positive changes that had already happened for her.

Marg was able to accept the events that had occurred in her family. She would never forget about them, and life would never be the same again. But she could go on from here feeling much better about herself and her parenting skills.

In her counseling, Marg had been supported to explore and accept the fact that her own parents had been physically abusive to her. They had been harmful to her emotionally and not provided her with role models for nurturing her own children. She came to see the ways in which her husband was able to alienate her from her daughter, who displaced her in her mother and wife roles without her understanding what was going on.

Marg gained insight into these family dynamics and was able to begin working on healthy role boundaries with her children and husband. She grew into her role as an empowered adult and parent. In counseling she eventually felt safe enough to talk about her own childhood sexual abuse for the first time and how it had affected her sexuality. Marg had left home after high school graduation to get married and had never worked outside the home. Now, with the help of friends, her counselor's support, and community resources, she was able to get a job and feel more independent.

Story #2: GINA

Gina comes from an ethnic and religious background that has strict teachings regarding a mother's role in a family. She believed that she is responsible for keeping the family intact and meeting the needs of everyone in the family. Shock and amazement overwhelmed Gina when a caseworker from the state Department of Social and Health Services and a policeman arrived on the doorstep of her comfortable middle-class home to tell her that her daughter had reported being sexually molested by her family.

Gina's immediate response was, "I don't believe it!" This resulted in her 10-year-old daughter's removal from the home and placement in foster care. Only when her husband had moved out of the house was her daughter allowed to return.

Depressed, Gina felt completely inadequate to cope alone with the daily demands and activities of her daughter and teenage son. She agonized over the fact that her daughter had talked to a stranger about her father's abuse instead of telling her. She struggled with the shame, feeling that she had failed not only as a parent but as a partner, excusing her husband's behavior because of her usual tiredness at the end of the day and her frequent lack of interest in having sex with him.

Her counselor respected her decision to remain with he husband and to work with him to rebuild the family with the help of their extended families. She was able to define new terms for a "healthy" family within these goals.

Story #3: SHIRLEY

Often the offender, while known to the family, is not a relative. Less often—but increasingly more common—the child is molested by an older child or sibling. This story emphasizes how a mother's still unresolved feelings about her own childhood sexual molestation is triggered by her daughter's abuse.

Shirley's 3-year-old daughter told her one night, during the child's regular bath, that while she was out playing in the apartment complex playground, a big boy she didn't know had told her to take off her clothes. He subsequently touched the child in her private area. Shirley was shocked, but she maintained a cool attitude and got a few more details from her daughter. As her child spoke to her, Shirley thought of another little girl, herself, who had been abused by her grandfather when she was three. The "touching" in her own childhood had happened on many occasions, and she still felt the shame and helplessness as she now tried to comfort her own little girl.

Shirley had never told anyone about her own abuse. One day, in a discussion with her daughter's therapist, she acknowledged that she, too, had been a victim. The therapist encouraged her to get her own counselor and work through her early childhood abuse so that she could feel better able to protect her own child and to improve her relationship with her husband. It seemed that there was a tension in her marriage that revolved around their sexual relationship. This had worsened since their daughter's abuse by the child's requests to sleep with them. She chose a counselor who was able to help her talk about her childhood molestation and her current fears and concerns.

This helped Shirley to deal with her daughter's abuse and to maintain the daughter's self-esteem by avoiding the guilt and confusion that Shirley had endured. Additionally, Shirley felt confident about talking to her husband about her abuse and how it had affected her sexually. They worked together to improve their sexual relationship.

Story #4: SUSAN

Susan was a rebellious adolescent who became bored with school and got involved with an older man. Against the wishes of her family, she married him when she was 18. After their son was born, Susan's relationship to her husband rapidly deteriorated. He exhibited bizarre behavior sexually, and he was cruel and abusive toward Susan, who was able to leave and return to her family of origin with her child. She still felt that was only fair that her 3-year-old son should have visitation with his father and was quite dismayed when he reported inappropriate sexual behavior on the part of his father during a visitation. This three-year-old was verbal and credible. Susan reported the situation to Child Protective Services (CPS), but it became a custody rather than a criminal case, owing to the age of the young child. Susan felt discounted by the various authorities, believing it was her own young age that kept her from being listened to. After another visit, her son reported explicit sexual behavior once again. She reported again to CPS, and this time the prosecutor filed charges.

However, the most difficult part for Susan was the fact that no real action had been taken with the first report. Having been ignored, she felt angry that her child had to go through the second molestation before any real action was taken. Compounding this was Susan's guilt at having let her child see the father again. Susan was supported by an advocate from the local sexual assault response center and was given information about the legal process. The advocate encouraged Susan to be assertive and to recognize the inherent difficulties in prosecuting suspected offenders in cases involving children as young as her own.

Susan's fears that her son's abuse may cause him to be homosexual were also addressed by the counselor, who provided information about sexual orientation and child sexual abuse.

It is important to emphasize that no two family situations are alike when counseling needs are considered.

References

Berliner, Lucy, and Elliott, Diane M. (1996). "Sexual Abuse of Children," *APSAC Handbook*. Thousand Oaks, CA: Sage.

Deblinger, Esther, Beliner, Lucy, and Heflin, Anne Hope. (1996). *Treating Sexually Abused Children and Their Non-offending Parents*. Thousand Oaks, CA: Sage.

8.

Parenting

This chapter tries to answer some of the common questions that mothers ask about their children who have been molested. It also provides anecdotes, advice, and other information that mothers have offered through the years.

COMMONLY ASKED QUESTIONS

Was this my child's fault?

No, it wasn't. Your child is innocent of blame and responsibility for what has happened.

Does my child need counseling?

Yes, by someone trained to work with sexually abused children. This is especially true for children who were molested repeatedly by one or more offenders.

How will the molestation affect my child?

It depends on a lot of things, including the child's age, knowledge of sexuality and abuse, the child's relationship with the offender, the particular form of abuse, the frequency of the abuse, the amount of support the child receives, etc.

While it is difficult to generalize, there are some patterns in a molested child's psychosocial development that are helpful to note. Children who are nonviolently molested once, and are supported by all the various parties once they have disclosed, may not suffer as serious emotional harm as a child who is molested more severely. A "more severely molested child" is one who is raped or molested with threats of violence, or who is repeatedly molested over a period of time.

Young children who are severely molested may exhibit withdrawal (or the opposite, erratic acting out), sexual interest beyond their age (e.g., frequent masturbation, interest in others' genitals, sexual talk), changes in appetite, regressive behavior (e.g., bed-wetting or thumb-sucking), disorientation, depression, and excessive neediness. Such children may also exhibit lack of trust toward others in general, or toward specific persons (the offender, for example); they may not want to be left with that person or near others who remind them of that person.

Older children may hate themselves. Eating disorders such as anorexia (self-starvation) and bulimia (self-induced vomiting) sometimes are associated with self-hatred and the wish to physically "disappear." Older children may also engage in other self-destructive behavior, such as running away, being truant, indulging in drugs and alcohol, attempting suicide, and sexual promiscuity. Be aware that the child's behavior may change over time, as the child matures. If a child was molested at a young age, she (or he) will begin to reflect on it in adolescence with new questions and concerns. Children molested in adolescence often do not want to talk about it for years, even though their behavior indicates they are seriously affected by what happened to them.

What will people say about my child's molestation?

It probably depends on who knows and how they learned about it. Even if you try to maintain confidentiality, others may find out. Therefore, it helps to develop some strategies for coping. The easiest comments from others to deal with are those made overtly to you or your child.

For example, Sylvia's adolescent daughter Renee came home from school on more than one occasion saying that the other kids had written "slut" and "whore" on her locker or called her these names in the hallway. Information of the abuse had spread through the school, and the daughter was being taunted. Sylvia helped her daughter to understand that what happened to her was not her fault. Then she and Renee had a long talk and explored why the offender (not a family member) had picked Renee (a vulnerable preadolescent) to take advantage of. This was a discussion they hadn't had before. They came up with some things Renee could say and do when the other kids made their cruel comments.

Did the child enjoy the sex?

Violent sexual acts of all kinds involving physical pain are not pleasurable. Sexual stimulation delivered more gently, especially if introduced gradually and with positive reinforcement, can be pleasurable. Some children say that the sex felt good. Others felt confused by the sensations and registered no definitive feeling. Others say they felt repulsion. However, even if sex felt good to the child, it was wrong and abusive for an adult (or even a teenager) to use the child for sexual gratification before the child is old enough to have mature understanding of sexuality and mutual consent.

Why is my child so angry at me?

Your child may have expected you to know she (or he) was molested or to have prevented it from happening. Research with incest survivors who were abused by their fathers shows that mothers often become the focus for feelings of anger, hatred, and other animosities. Daughters may even treat their mothers with contempt. Most children hold their mothers responsible for the abuse, rather than the offender who committed the acts. Mothers in incestuous families are oftentimes not powerful, and the child finds it easier to blame someone less powerful than the offender (whom the child may idealize for his power and authority).

Angry behavior on the child's part toward you will require a good counselor to address this. Bonds and trust must be reestablished—both require time and commitment, since they may have been damaged years ago and need much repair. The child and mother have some learning to do with regard to family dynamics, respect for each other's role in the family, and so forth. This process is often slow and difficult, but competent counselors can help.

Has my child contracted a venereal disease or other medical problems, as a result of the molestation?

Possibly. Only a check-up by a sensitive physician will tell for sure. Sometimes children worry about their bodies in general after they have been molested. They need to be reassured that they are all right. Be sure that the physician has had training in treating sexual abuse victims, and advise her or him about the problem you are dealing with.

How will the molestation affect my other children?

The other children may feel different from the child who has been victimized. They may also develop feelings of jealousy toward the child who is "getting so much attention." Or they may be confused about what has happened and/or where they fit in. Sometimes, they may be empathetic and supportive, depending on your children's ages and how much they understand about the molestation. Talk to all of your children and give them age-appropriate factual information. Keep them updated as new events occur to help them understand why their sibling is getting so much attention. Try to plan activities that allow the child who was molested to be involved in the same way as the other children.

Will my child have sexual problems?

Your child may have a lot of feelings and fears about sex that children of their age typically do not. You can help your child by reinforcing the notion that sexual experiences can be positive when they occur among persons of similar age and maturity. Children emerging from incest experiences are already highly sexualized and may seek sexual relations with others at an earlier age than adolescents usually do. In this case, you may want to initiate discussions about sexual responsibility, protection from venereal disease and pregnancy, and other issues. On the other hand, some molested children grow up with an aversion to sex—a response of a different sort. In either case, professional counseling is important to help the child develop perspective and a healthy sense of her (or his) sexual self.

How much should we talk about the molestation?

The molestation often occupies center stage at home for several weeks or months, even though it may not always be talked about. It's on everyone's minds. It will be important to keep facts about your child's legal case out in the open so everyone knows what's happening, but how and when you present that information should be carefully planned. You may need to make a "space" away from other distractions to sit down with your children and explain new developments. Let the molested child speak for herself, if she is old enough and wants to do this. If counseling is a part of the follow-up, it may be helpful to exchange information about this. For example, "Tonight we need to talk about the new ground rules for our family that we've been working on in counseling," or "Stacey (the victim) has been learning about speaking up for herself this week." The other children may want to ask questions or to express their feelings. These family chats should happen every week or so in the beginning, but less often as time goes on. You can play it by ear to some extent. Ask your children if the molestation is being talked about too much, if this is your worry.

Is there anyone outside the family we should tell about the molestation?

Presumably, quite a few already know, if the case has been reported and is proceeding through some kind of legal or therapeutic process. So, in a sense, you already have experience talking to non-family members about the abuse. But there are still others you may want to consider talking to. Teachers and anyone else who has regular contact with your child will find it helpful to know about the child's abuse. You can ask these people to respect your child's privacy by not telling others, if you want. Beyond these essential people, it is you and your child's decision whom to tell. Make sure every member of the immediate family is aware of how the information about the abuse will be handled. Keep in mind, however, that word typically gets out no matter what you do. It's useful to anticipate this and to have a coping strategy in mind. One possibility is to consider being more "open" in general about what has occurred. This can be part of a process of getting rid of the sexual secrets that have been harmful to your child, yourself, and your family. It's also an approach that gives you some control over information that's circulated—in other words, facts instead of rumor. But openness may not be something you are ready for yet. Use your own sense of things.

Will our family ever be normal and happy again?

Yes, and you can contribute to that normalcy. Begin to maintain regular household routines as soon as possible (e.g., chores, schedules, celebrations, mealtimes, etc.). Maintain discipline guidelines (hopefully these do not involve physical force). Praise and reward your children when appropriate. Try to be consistent with your rules and praise, instead of erratic. Work on communicating openly and honestly about thoughts and feelings.

QUESTIONS PARTICULAR TO
MOTHERS IN INCESTUOUS FAMILIES

Why do I feel jealousy toward my daughter?

Probably because you have unconsciously come to feel that your daughter is your competitor for your husband's (or partner's) affection. Or you feel that because he chose her, she is more attractive than you are. You may have developed these feelings because the offender helped to generate such ideas. It serves his motives to have you and your daughter at odds. She is more likely to side with him and be loyal to him if she is fighting with you or senses your disapproval of her. Jealousy toward the daughter is very typical for mothers living in incestuous families. But it is also unhealthy for you and your child(ren). Remember, your child has been molested at a young and vulnerable age, and she bears no responsibility for this. Seek counseling to try and convert your feelings of jealousy to anger toward the offender.

Can my child and husband have a normal relationship again?

Well, remember when you ask this that they have not *really* had a "normal" father-child relationship since the first time the father fantasized having sex with the child! They can establish a *new* relationship, with strict ground rules for interaction, with the help of long-term counseling and regular monitoring by someone outside the family. However, some father-child relationships are permanently damaged and can never be salvaged after the molestation. Your child will need to make her or his own decision about this relationship when she or he is old enough to do so.

How do we establish trust and openness in our family?

By beginning to express thoughts and feelings to your children and helping them to express theirs to you and to each other. By sharing the ordinary things that you did that day with them. By setting aside time each day to listen to them. You do not have to divulge your deepest thoughts with your children, but share those things that will help them to understand why you feel and act as you do. Let everyone know that what happened is wrong and that the child was not to blame. Reinforce the importance of not keeping secrets from each other any more. Bring your children into family decision-making whenever possible. Observe respect and boundaries with each other around feelings and sexuality.

ADDITIONAL NOTES
ON PARENTING

Most of us raise our children the way that we were raised—in other words, philosophies and practices in parenting are passed down to us from our parents. In the process, we may or may not have gotten what we need to successfully parent our children in today's world—even under the best of conditions. All parents today are up against challenges that did not exist in earlier times. Peer groups form earlier and have increasing influence on children's ideas and behaviors, such as early experimentation with alcohol, drugs, and sex, as well as other exciting and rebellious activity. Television, films, rock music, and other mass media stimulate children and adolescents to be "cool" and act like adults at earlier ages. So if your child is sexually molested, your parenting skills to cope with these and the new difficulties are not only tested but strained. You will have a million questions, and each day you will be confronted by behavior that you will wonder, "Was this caused by the child's abuse?"

There can be no better support than for you than to find a mother's group made up of other women whose children have also been molested. These women are going through the same things that you are. If your local women's shelter, rape crisis center, or mental health clinic doesn't already have such a group, ask the staff if they would consider forming one. Your own support through such a group is critical for your survival. Over the long run, it will be the daily trials and tribulations that will be your toughest challenge. You will need other mothers to talk to on a continuous basis. You can be totally honest with others who have been through the same things that you have, and you can also gain satisfaction in offering them your support. Such groups work smoothest with a neutral facilitator—a trained counselor for instance—who can keep the discussion going and make sure that no one person dominates the group. Facilitators can also raise questions to ponder and can provide background information about child molestation available through research or legal sources. You may be asked to pay a nominal amount at each group meeting to help pay for the facilitator's time or the rent on the place you meet.

Individual counseling can also contribute much to your healing, as the previous chapter discusses. However, it is through a group of women who share your own concerns and experiences that you may find the most important bonding and can draw the greatest inspiration and practical advice. Most mothers need individual counseling as well as support groups to pull through after the molestation of their children.

The argument that all mothers are complicit in father-daughter incest is refuted by numerous examples of mothers who, upon discovering the incest, react with shock, outrage and prompt action in defense of their daughters.

Judith Herman
associate clinical professor
of Psychiatry
Harvard Medical School*

---

* Judith Herman (with Lisa Hirschman), "Father-Daughter Incest," in P.B. Bart and E. G. Moran, *Violence Against Women: The Bloody Footprints*. Newbury Park, CA: Safe Publications, p. 49.

Further Reading

Adams, Caren, and Fay, Jennifer. (1989. *Free of the Shadows: Recovering from Sexual Violence*. Oakland, CA: Harbinger Publications.

Ashley, Sandi (Ed.). (1992). *The Missing Voice: Writings by Mothers of Incest Victims*. Dubuque, IA: Kendall/Hunt Publishing Co.

Berliner, Lucy, and Elliott, Diana M. (1996). "Sexual Abuse of Children," *APSAC Handbook*. Thousand Oaks, CA: Sage Publications.

Buckwald, Emilie; Fletcher, Pamela R.; and Roth, Martha. (1993) *Transforming a Rape Culture*. Minneapolis, MN: Milkweed Productions.

Burns, Maryviolet C. (Ed.). (1986). *The Speaking Profits Us: Violence in the Lives of Women of Color*. Seattle, WA: Center for the Prevention of Sexual and Domestic Violence.

Deblinger, Esther, and Heflin, Anne Hope. (1996). *Treating Sexually Abused Children and Their Non-Offending Parents*. Thousand Oaks, CA: Sage Publications.

Fortune, Marie M. (1989). *Is Nothing Sacred? When Sex Invades the Pastoral Relationship*. San Francisco, CA: Harper & Row.

Fortune, Marie. (1983). *Sexual Violence: The Unmentionable Sin*. Pilgrim Press.

Gordon, Linda. (1988). *Heroes of their Own Lives: The Politics and History of Family Violence*. New York, NY: Penguin Books.

Herman, Judith (with Lisa Hirshman). (1993). "Father-Daughter Incest," in P.B. Bart and E.G. Moran, *Violence Against Women: The Bloody Footprints*. Newbury Park, CA: Sage Publications.

Hunter, Mic. (1990). *Abused Boys: The Neglected Victims of Sexual Abuse*. Lexington, MA: Lexington Books.

MacFarlane, Kee, and Waterman, Jill. (1986). *Sexual Abuse of Young Children*. New York, NY: Guilford Press.

Orr, Tracy. (1995). *No Right Way: The Voices of Mothers of Incest Survivors*. London, ENG: Scarlet Press.

Strong, Marilee. (1997). "Monsters in Our Midst," World Wide Web (*http://www.diablopubs.com/focus/ARCHIVES/FEATURES/sexoffenders.html*).

The Author

Carolyn M. Byerly, Ph.D., teaches journalism and international communication at Ithaca College in Ithaca, New York. She is the author of articles on news coverage of sexual assault and domestic violence. She is also a community activist. Since the late 1970s, she has been involved locally, nationally, and internationally with groups that support victims and survivors of sexual and domestic violence.

ORDER FORM
for additional copies of
THE MOTHER'S BOOK

Name _____

Organization _____

Address _____
(street)

_____
(city)   (state)   (zip)

Phone   Home: (   ) _____

             Work: (   ) _____

Number of copies _____ @ $7.95 per copy $_____

Shipping/handling costs: 1 copy $3.00
                            2-10 copies $6.00 $_____

Washington state residents add 8.6% sales tax $_____

                            TOTAL enclosed $_____

ORDERS MUST BE PREPAID. Make check payable to CPSDV.
Mail to:

**Center for the Prevention of
Sexual and Domestic Violence (CPSDV)**
936 N. 34th Street, Suite 200
Seattle, WA 98103
(206) 634-1903   FAX (206) 634-0115

<u>BULK ORDERS</u>:
For 11 or more copies, please order directly from Kendall/Hunt Publishing
Company at (800) 228-0810. Bulk discounts are available.

 *The Center for the Prevention of Sexual and Domestic
Violence is a private, nonprofit, interreligious educational
organization whose mission is to end sexual and domestic
violence by working through churches, synagogues, and
seminaries in the United States, Canada, and around the
world. See our new homepage at: http://www.cpsdv.org*